W9-BUV-430

NINE WAYS WOMEN SABOTAGE
THEIR CAREERS

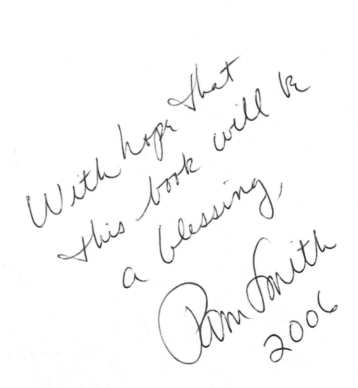

With hope that
this book will be
a blessing,

Pam Smith
2006

Nine Ways Women Sabotage Their Careers

Their Careers

*Real World Experiences That Will Change
the Way Women Manage Their Professional Lives*

PAMELA J. SMITH

Copyright © 2004 by Pamela J. Smith.

Library of Congress Number: 2004095292

ISBN : Softcover 1-4134-6400-9

All rights reserved. No part of this book may be reproduced or transmitted in any
form or by any means, electronic or mechanical, including photocopying,
recording, or by any information storage and retrieval system,
without permission in writing from the author.

This book was printed in the United States of America.

CONTENTS

ACKNOWLEDGEMENTS

First and foremost, this book would have remained unwritten without the encouragement and support of my husband, Steve Smith. He is a man among men.

The editing done by my dear friend, Lois Swagerty, made all the difference in my ability to transform the ideas in my head into the book in your hands.

The cover design by Audrey Verso gave life to the title and represented the finishing touch on the project.

Without my mentors, my business life story would have been a very different one, filled with trial and error, with emphasis on the error.

And, without God in my life, I'd be a total mess.

INTRODUCTION

Avoiding the Chutes While Climbing the Ladders

A woman's career is much like the children's board game that requires each player to maneuver through a labyrinth of chutes and ladders to get to the next level. Some career decisions can launch a woman up the ladder to a new level of success. Some career decisions, however, can propel her down one of those irritating chutes, causing her to retrace her steps over previously covered territory.

A slide down a chute is not always caused by a career decision. A woman can sometimes find herself slipping down a chute due to a change in circumstances, environment, or company strategy in which she had very little say or input.

If you remember the goal of the board game, it is the player's hope to avoid as many of the chutes as possible, especially the largest chute which places the player well back in the game. In the board game, avoiding the chutes and leveraging the ladders depends on the player's luck in the roll of the dice.

A woman's career is much like this game. While a little luck certainly helps, the number of slides down the chutes can be reduced and the number of available ladders can be increased through wise choices. To avoid chutes you need to recognize what the top of each slippery slide looks like. To increase access to the available ladders you need to avoid the chutes.

Mistakes are inevitable when moving forward in a career; they are also a necessary part of progress as they teach us valuable lessons. Most mistakes are merely a small section of rough road on an otherwise smooth career path. Mistakes can have a positive effect in stimulating new ways of thinking and can even reveal a hidden ladder which leads to a new direction for success.

Some mistakes, however, have a great negative impact on a woman's career. Some slowly erode a career, causing her to move farther and farther away from her career goals. Other mistakes occur on such a grand scale that they sharply terminate a career path.

As women progress in their careers they will discover that packaged along with the standard challenges and obstacles to success are special dynamics that apply only to women. Successful women understand those dynamics and use them to their advantage.

My husband has listened to many stories from my business career. Because he knows my intense desire to help women avoid unnecessary career pitfalls, he encouraged me to put into print what I have learned through my own experiences and have observed in the experiences of others. As I share stories about women leaders, I do it with a deep respect for the decisions they have made, the course corrections they have taken, and the obstacles they have overcome as they traveled on their unique career paths.

Just as a board game player refers to a rulebook to learn game strategy, a career woman will find it helpful to refer to a guidebook as she develops work and life strategies. I have included a few pearls of practical wisdom from the New International Version of the Bible, which I refer to as the Guidebook. While the Bible may seem to be an unusual reference book for business, I have found sound advice within it that transcends time and culture. The Guidebook also contains many leadership examples, some that are good ones to emulate and others that serve as models to avoid.

In the business world in which a woman lives each day there is an abundance of unwritten rules containing hidden pitfalls that lead directly to an appropriately sized chute. This book breaks the secret codes and reveals why many women fail to achieve their career goals. I have written this book in the hope that it will enable women to discover and avoid behaviors that cause them to sabotage their careers.

Some situations in this book may validate what you've suspected, some may surprise you, some may challenge you, and some may reveal a red flag that you've never before considered. No matter where you stand on your career ladder or no matter how far down a chute you may have slid, you can resume progress up the career ladder of choice by eliminating behaviors that sabotage your success.

*   *   *

SABOTAGE #1

Key Concepts

- A woman sabotages her career when she views qualities unique to her gender as business weaknesses
- A woman needs to make peace with the business world's double standard
- A woman who views her uniqueness as weakness gives men permission to do the same

SABOTAGE #1

Viewing Uniqueness as Weakness

What's So Unique about Women?

Women have been created with distinct qualities that manifest themselves in their leadership styles and in their approaches to business challenges. A woman's gender distinctions are not business weaknesses, yet many women choose to view them in that way. Women who desire to have successful careers need to understand, manage, and leverage gender uniqueness.

For example, I have observed that while men tend to focus on a single issue at a time, women can multitask and can process information flooding in simultaneously from multiple sources. When a woman effectively manages her multitasking skill, she leverages her skill as a strength and can achieve a large number and a wide variety of results that support her objectives. However, if she fails to channel her multitasking skill toward key goals, she repositions her skill as a weakness and her male colleagues will view her as not being focused.

The way that most women develop solutions is distinct from that of their men colleagues. Men tend to be linear thinkers who reach a decision by connecting related thoughts through a straight-line sequential process. Women tend to be spatial thinkers who consider an issue from many different perspectives that may even appear to be unrelated before coming to the same decision.

As spatial thinkers, women can have a difficult time communicating their decision-making process to linear-thinking men. A male manager often finds it difficult to appreciate that a female manager can come to the same business conclusion as he did, but by using such a different thought process. I can so clearly remember the puzzled look that came over a particular senior manager's face the first time that

I explained how I reached an important business conclusion. Even though he agreed with and accepted my solution, he expressed frustration over what he viewed as my around-the-world way of getting to the recommendation. After a time he came to accept that the process I used didn't really matter as long as I delivered results.

Women are unique in their ability to nurture. When a woman manager views her nurturing ability as a strength, she demonstrates appropriate compassion to employees and becomes an excellent developer of human capital. She becomes a superior trainer, mentor, and instructor. However, when a woman in management views nurturing as something that mothers do only with children, she will perceive nurturing as a business weakness and will find herself surrounded by employees who aren't developing and who aren't contributing toward achievement of goals.

Women possess a number of other distinct qualities that enable them to be excellent managers. For example, women are strongly perceptive, so much so that they have their own special term to describe the phenomenon: "women's intuition." When women use their intuition as part of the hiring process they often key in quickly on the perfect candidate.

I have observed that women with people management responsibilities can lead larger teams and can handle a wider span of control than men managers. Women managers value loyalty, give loyalty, and develop loyalty among team members. What a great management package!

Nonetheless, despite being equipped with the power of gender uniqueness, many talented women head directly for the nearest chute by choosing to view their unique qualities as weaknesses, especially when they move into a management environment where men managers occupy the significant majority position. They begin to doubt that their gender traits will contribute to their future success. It's as though someone throws a switch that turns on a flashing hypnotic message: "Must act like men to succeed. Must act like men to succeed."

A woman manager begins to sabotage her own career when
she becomes convinced that talents unique to her gender are
business weaknesses to be avoided at all costs.

Don't Join the Actor's Guild

Are there still companies where women are treated differently than men who have similar if not the same job responsibilities? Absolutely! Are there companies that have made strategic decisions to limit the number of women that are hired into key positions? No question about it! Does a double standard still exist in the business world? Without a doubt!

This is the business environment in which many career women find themselves. It is a climate that pressures a woman to become an actor: she concludes that if she acts just like a male leader would, she will somehow eliminate the double standard and will become part of the male majority. When a woman buys into the idea of acting as much as possible like the men, she sabotages her leadership impact. She abandons the attributes that can give her the edge over men colleagues because she views and treats the uniqueness that she brings to the leadership team as weakness. And if she treats her distinguished abilities as weaknesses, so will her men colleagues when those abilities instinctively reveal themselves.

I truly believe that many companies are unaware that a double standard is encouraged by their management practices. I also believe that women should educate those companies and work toward changing those practices. Change often comes slowly; therefore, women need to decide how they will conduct themselves in their current company climate. The sooner a woman who steps into a leadership position in a company that promotes a double standard work environment makes her peace with it, the happier and more successful she will be.

In a climate where men are treated with favor many career women feel that the more they imitate the work styles of the men, the better will be their chance to advance. Women often strive hard to be viewed as "one of the boys." They adopt a strategy of likeness, thinking that by imitating the male behaviors, they will improve their chances to be incorporated into the group as equals. This strategy can produce an opposite effect.

Women who attempt to behave like men often make poor choices. I worked with two women new to management who decided that if they spent an evening puffing on cigars with the male managers, the men would more readily accept them. The men helped and encouraged the women nonsmokers to puff away. The next morning, both women were visibly nauseated by the aftereffect of the cigars. The men enjoyed a hearty laugh at the women's expense. This was not the outcome the women managers had hoped for.

Perception is Everything

Women in leadership positions have a true dilemma. While they bring a wonderful uniqueness in style and approach to the team, the men leaders often have a difficult time in understanding and accepting their distinct package. When faced with resistance, many women begin to perceive their unique attributes as weaknesses that need to be changed or hidden if they are to make strides in a work world where men seem to control all the rules, regulations, processes, and procedures.

> *When women start to view their uniqueness as weakness, they give their male colleagues permission to view them in the same way.*

Dealing with the "Boys' Club"

"It's a boys' club and everybody knows it; how do you stand it?"

This question was posed to me by a middle manager and speaks to the frustration felt by those who witness how women in management positions can be set apart and treated differently by the men on the management team. Having had personal experience working in such a climate, I can attest that boys' clubs do exist and that it is challenging to excel within that type of environment. The higher the level of management that a woman achieves the more likely she is to find a boys' club. What has surprised me is not the number of women managers who are upset over experiencing discriminatory behaviors, but rather the number of male managers who are appalled that boys' clubs are alive and well. In fact, it was a male manager who asked me how I could stand it.

Boys' club franchises are not just alive and well; they continue to multiply. A male department head expressed to me his great concern over the boys'-club atmosphere that had been established by the new management. The opinions of the women in leadership positions were being discounted and ignored. The situation was causing women to reconsider if they should be investing their futures with the organization.

Thankfully, not all companies sponsor such clubs. There are good companies to be found that offer women an equal and level management environment. But in those companies where clubs do thrive, there is always a club leader, usually the highest-ranking executive in the group. It is he who demonstrates the rules to the other members who are then expected to conform to those rules. There are even rules for outside-the-office activities. If the club leader golfs, all members are expected to golf, but not better than the club leader. If the club leader enjoys baseball, all members are expected to watch the games of, and root for, the preferred professional team of the leader.

The club's very foundation is disturbed when the club leader decides to host a female manager. I use the word "host" because in companies that sponsor a boys' club women are rarely permitted to become full members with all rights and privileges. Sometimes an invitation is extended under pressure to get a female in place so that the company can look good on its EEO report. Other times, the club leader desires to take a step toward embracing diversity and wants to see if a woman manager's unique set of attributes will provide greater balance to the team. The club members can feel tense and even threatened by the upcoming change to their club environment.

What Really Happens?

Once granted entry into the clubhouse, a woman leader attempts to assimilate quickly. Especially at the senior management club level, a woman makes the critical career error of observing and then imitating the behaviors of the male members, even behaviors that she finds offensive. She puts aside the characteristics that bring value and make her such a great asset when she tries to mimic the tactics, language, humor, and style of the club members as she seeks acceptance.

This makes the club members happy. They are very pleased to see that she won't be causing any problems; the dust settles, the threat subsides, and the male members continue business as usual. She makes no real impact and finds herself forever positioned on the periphery, which makes the male club members feel safe. The male members may even nominate her to be the regular note taker for business meetings because of her excellent skill in producing accurate meeting minutes. As she becomes frustrated with how she is being treated by the club and eventually voices her displeasure, the club leader will take note of her poor attitude and will begin to seek ways to cancel her membership.

Can a Woman Ever Be "Just One of the Boys"?

At a company where I once worked, the senior management level formed a boys' club. In time a woman joined the executive staff. Although she did not golf, she soon discovered that the boys' club leader was an accomplished golfer. Since all of the club members were golfers, she decided to take a few golf lessons in an attempt to become accepted by the club. She would discuss her progress with the boys' club members, who had a field day laughing behind her back when she mentioned such activities as "learning to hit the ball out of those sand piles."

At a company-sponsored golf tournament, she presented herself in full (and beautiful, I might add) golf regalia. The executive men formed themselves into foursomes. Her name was nowhere in sight. The woman executive was teamed with three lower level women managers who had also bought into the idea that playing in the golf event would help their career advancement with the company (I have to admit that I was one of them). The all-female group was positioned as the last to tee off.

The female executive clubbed her way around the golf course to the grand amusement of the men. The scorekeeper stopped counting her strokes and listed a "10" on each hole. Our group was so far behind that we agreed it was best to stop after the ninth hole. At the awards banquet that followed the golf event, she and her team were called up to receive the "best dressed team" award, which was hastily created by the boys' club and was presented with much snickering.

Unless a woman is an accomplished golfer, racquetball player, or whatever the club leader activity of choice, she will lessen her impact by trying to act like one. A couple of lessons will not equip a woman to compete at the skill level of men who have played the game for many years.

Whether or not a women leader should golf seems to be an unsettling issue for many women. I know a few women who enjoy playing golf, but the majority of women have expressed to me that they have little desire to play, but feel pressured by male counterparts who insist that women hurt their careers when they opt out of the annual company golf event. My experience indicates that whether a woman chooses to play in such events or chooses to decline, her decision has no bearing on career advancement.

When I stepped up to an upper middle management position, the golf issue reared its head again. I recognized that in order to golf at the level that the men managers could, I would have to invest a fair amount of money and a significant amount of time doing something that I honestly wouldn't enjoy. I made a strategic decision to inform the club members that during their golf outings, I'd be at the spa. They would enjoy time on the links; I would tremendously enjoy the down time from my hectic work schedule. The club members were relieved that I wouldn't be slowing them down on the course due to my low skill level. When the opportunity presented itself, my golf skills (or lack of them) had no bearing on my promotion to senior management.

Despite warnings I had received from some of the club members that lots of deals were cut on the golf course and that I'd be missing out, I found that while some deals indeed were made during golf activities, the majority of the negotiations that really impacted the business were completed in an office or over a meal. Whenever I needed to negotiate with a client who enjoyed golfing, there was an ample supply of male club members who were eager to help. While I specialized in customer relationship development at the office and over dinner, my male counterparts handled the sports activities and had a chance to bond with the customer as well: a true win-win scenario for the company and for me.

Eventually the club leader who loved golf so much moved on. The replacement club leader was a runner, not a golfer. The members of the boys club found that golf became a stealth activity referred to as an offsite meeting. A few years later, I changed organizations to one headed by a president with no passion for golf, but with a great love for fishing. The bottom line is: golf if you like it, don't golf if it is not your passion. Build a reputation based on business skills, not a golf score.

Do We Validate the Bias?

Women, particularly those in management positions, will be exposed to many actions of men in leadership positions that demonstrate biased thinking. When men managers who are used to a primarily male staff find themselves having to deal with a new female manager, they are forced to step out of their comfort zone—a zone that is deep, wide, and well guarded. Men in leadership, especially at the senior management level, have long ago settled on the terms of interaction with each other. They function as similar units with similar approaches to the business process. They don't need to get to know each other at a deep level in order to understand each other. It is only natural that they would have a difficult time when a woman manager invades their society.

A woman who accepts a leadership position needs to view her appointment as one that carries a hidden obligation. Whether or not she realizes it, a woman who achieves a high-level management position sets the standard by which other women model their professional behavior. Women who aspire to have career paths that include key leadership roles will emulate her. She will also be watched carefully by men managers in key leadership positions. Her conduct will either convince the men's management society that it is safe to open up to women leaders, or it will solidify biased thinking against placing women in positions of impact.

The male president of a company openly shared with me that the behavior of a woman manager who holds a key company position has poisoned his male executive staff against considering females for additional upper level management positions. She is a terrific worker and the president speaks highly of her work quality and company loyalty. However, her attitude has earned her a reputation of being impossible to get along with, moody, and disrespectful to senior management. During her annual review she receives high ratings on work output, but continues to receive a low rating for team interaction. She is not interested in an upwardly moving career path; her work goal is to continue in the position she has while increasing her pay status.

I see this woman manager as someone who doesn't match her actions to her goal. By disrespecting the president and the others within her company, she limits her ability to maximize her annual pay increase, which she says is important. But more than just working against her own goal, her behavior is sabotaging the opportunities within her company that might have been filled with good women leaders.

Tactically Speaking: What Works? What Doesn't?

Knowing what to do is just as important as knowing what not to do. I have found that **creativity** works well when a woman is seeking acceptance. When I crossed over into marketing management, my new boss played it safe by giving this new and untested female product manager three product lines that were considered "dogs." I didn't hear "dogs"; I heard "challenges."

I knew that I first had to get the selling team excited over the products. Understanding how sales representatives thrive on competition, I decided to create training programs that required each rep to compete in various games. One game was a mix-and-match-the-parts contest that made the complex nature of the products simple. Another was a game show competition that cemented the key points of the products in the sales reps' memories.

Senior management questioned my methods at first, but after reviewing the results, congratulated me on my unique approach. All three product lines significantly exceeded quota for the first time in years, which earned me a top management award complete with club-issued jacket and lapel pin. It wasn't long before I was promoted to a higher level of management.

I have also found that **humor** works. When I moved into upper level sales management, I had full responsibility for the content of meetings that involved sales reps. For my first sales meeting as a vice president, I created commercials and short humorous training videos. I established a group of awards that I called the "Pammys" to recognize fun and somewhat bizarre achievements from the prior year, and presented them with the fanfare of a "Grammys" presentation night.

The relatively new company leader thought I was completely off-the-wall, and predicted disaster. I asked him to trust me. The meeting was a success. After the meeting concluded, he wanted to know how he could be the recipient of a "Pammy" and campaigned heavily to be in the following year's video productions.

Tough language *doesn't* work. Some of the techniques that women think are effective as a lower or middle manager really aren't, and don't transition well to the senior management level. A female supervisor in a plant operations leadership position was respected for her ability to solve technical problems, but was hated by most of her subordinates due to the rough language she felt she needed to use in her blue-collar environment. A male manager who interacted with her stated that he hadn't heard such rude and crude language since he had been in the military.

Eventually she was promoted to the upper management level. Mistakenly thinking that the boys in the club would identify with her communication method that was peppered with four letter expletives, she never adjusted her style to a more professional way of speaking. She soon disappeared from the company career-path radar screen. Professional language is the language that facilitates career growth.

Using Uniqueness to Achieve Results

I have discovered that the most significant way to be accepted and respected by the boys' club is to emphasize and achieve results. By achieving personal and company goals that add value to her organization, a woman manager will maximize her worth not only in her present position, but also in the future when she prepares for her next career move. A woman in management must resist the temptation to be assimilated through compromise of her unique skills and abilities, and must leverage her full influence by standing out with excellence in both performance and attitude.

At the lower- and middle-management levels, I found that I could establish a niche position as a generalist while my male counterparts were concentrating on being specialists. I decided that my best shot for upward career movement was to develop deep product knowledge and a broad range of transferable business skills. I sought out and participated in cross-functional team projects, as long as they didn't compromise my ability to achieve the goals for which I'd be held accountable at review time, so that I could broaden my KSA's (Knowledge, Skills, and Abilities). I am still amazed at the impact that being a generalist made in the series of promotions that were presented to me as I climbed the corporate ladder. Door after door was opened. I was always being asked to consider this or that position because of what one company president expressed as my "tribal knowledge."

However, when I took the step into senior management, I found it necessary to find a new niche. I needed to abandon the generalist strategy in favor of becoming a specialist. One of my senior management opportunities was facilitated by a notable set of international marketplace skills that I had developed years earlier. If I hadn't been that generalist years before, I wouldn't have qualified for the specialist role.

I have found that creativity counts when carving out a niche. One of the highest-ranking women in a large technology company that I am familiar with carved out her niche by making a successful high-level career out of managing low-profile projects. Once referred to as the "leader of doomed projects," she began tackling high-risk, under-funded projects. She skillfully kept them on a respirator until the decision was made to pull the plug or until she obtained adequate resources to breathe new life into them. Her ability to resuscitate key projects became critical to the company's progress in its markets.

The Most Unique Player on the Team

The significance of a woman's uniqueness can be illustrated through a baseball analogy. Picture a male manager as the pitcher and a female manager as the catcher. The pitcher often believes that the game depends only on his actions. He might not even appreciate the importance of the catcher. The catcher, who has a unique vantagepoint on the game, is critical to the pitcher's success in communicating what pitch to throw and where to throw it.

Sometimes the pitcher still thinks he knows best and decides to use a pitch that is different from what the catcher recommended; even then the catcher still has the responsibility for positioning the target so that the pitcher throws effectively. The catcher makes the pitcher successful. The catcher not only has to work with a different starting pitcher every game, but also has to manage the communication with the relief pitchers when they are put in the game as a result of the starting pitcher having a bad day.

Where would those pitchers be without that catcher? The catcher is just as much of an athlete as is any other member of the team. But the catcher is unique in the skills and equipment required to play the position well and is the only team member who sees and plays the game from a unique perspective. The team's success depends on the skill that the catcher brings to the team. If a woman on a male-dominated management team can picture herself in that important catcher's position, she'll understand how much value her unique perspective can bring to the team.

Celebrate Uniqueness

When it comes to understanding that a woman's uniqueness has been strategically placed in her, there is no better place to look than in what I call the original Guidebook for career success, the Holy Bible. In it are found two concepts that can help women to understand how God views them as they function in the workplace.

First, when God created the female differently from the male he used Adam's rib (Genesis 2:22). This gives us a picture that woman is to function side by side with the man in the completion of assigned work, using her unique attributes to complete the work process.

Secondly, a woman needs to know that she was "fearfully and wonderfully made" (Psalm 139:14b). She wasn't a mistake, and in fact, was made *fearfully*, meaning that she was fashioned to be so incredibly unique and special by God that she should live in awe and with great respect for her Creator. When a woman understands that she has been fully equipped with exactly what she needs and does not need to find substitutes she is empowered to use that uniqueness to its fullest as the strength it was intended to be.

To be successful, women need to celebrate their unique qualities and to use them with excellence. Women must choose whether or not they will allow the existence of a double standard to prevent them from career advancement. They must also choose how they will conduct themselves in a fraternity environment. Smart career women choose to conduct themselves in a way that opens more doors to women leaders in the future. The key to a woman's advancement in a double-standard-driven business world is not in exchanging her gender-related qualities for a phony presence; it is in developing new strengths and integrating them into her own unique approach.

*Uniqueness becomes a weakness only when
a woman chooses to ignore its strength.*

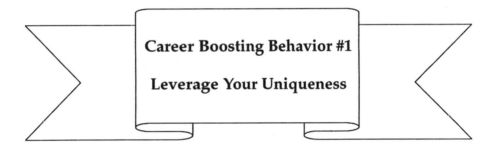

Career Boosting Behavior #1

Leverage Your Uniqueness

SABOTAGE #2

Key Concepts

- Women need to study men and use observations as success tools
- Women control how they react to the behaviors of men
- Women confuse male colleagues by inconsistent behavior

SABOTAGE #2

Neglecting to Treat Male Colleagues as Customers

Understanding Your Customer

At one time in the world's history the perfect man-and-woman relationship existed. It was a time when a man and woman completely understood each other and knew how to interact between each other with perfection. Unfortunately, the perfect communication of man and woman ended in the Garden of Eden when the serpent enticed Eve with the forbidden fruit. Male-female relationships have never been the same since.

Women know themselves, and therefore understand that women are bent toward certain behaviors. Women don't need to study other women. However, to be successful in a male-dominated management society, I have found that women need to picture themselves as top saleswomen who approach male colleagues as if they were customers from whom they want to get a positive buying decision. In order to treat men as customers, women need to study them to learn what motivates, what frustrates, and what elicits a positive response to their proposals and ideas.

The high achievers who were part of sales teams that I managed studied their customers to find out what made them tick. They learned each customer's operational language so that they could predict customer behaviors and manage opportunities. If the sales reps could anticipate the customer's objections, they could close the sale in the fastest possible time period.

There are male customers in authority over you, there are male customers who are your peers, and there are male customers in subordination to you. The more you can anticipate the behaviors of

27

your male colleagues, the better you can achieve your goals by working with them, around them, or through them.

*You might not be able to control the behaviors of men colleagues, but you **can** control your reaction to their behaviors.*

Style Plays a Role

Differences in style become magnified at the management level. All managers have leadership characteristics that fall into one of four styles. While most managers have some combination of styles, one style usually governs most of their demonstrated characteristics. The style names may differ depending on the instrument being used to determine a person's personality pattern, but in summary they include a controlling style, an expressive style, an analytical style, and an amiable style.

Most of the senior level male leaders with whom I have interacted had a predominantly controlling style. Generally speaking, controllers tend to disregard human capital. In their minds, other people are there to manage the employees, not them. They are usually unsympathetic, Machiavellian, and have an almost compulsive need to manage results through constant change. Controlling styles are often strong willed people who are decisive and focus on goal achievement. Failure is not an option; they want you to either get on board or get out of the way. Controllers don't want you to bother them with details; they just want to hear that the goal was met. They care about the bottom line, and they want you to get there quickly.

Expressive leaders can be great fun to work for, but often they don't follow through on commitments. They really do mean what they say when they say it, but then they often forget their obligations. They have an amazing talent for getting others to do almost anything for them. The expressive style leaders with whom I have interacted have led some of the most entertaining and exciting business meetings I've ever attended. The business part of the meeting lasted about three hours each business day; the rest of the time was fun-in-the-sun time. Expressives get bored and need constant stimulation.

Analytical leaders will leave you in awe over their ability to dissect problems. However, they will often spend so much time analyzing and planning that they never move the project forward. They seem standoffish and have high standards that are difficult to measure up to. Analyticals want all the details. In any selling situation the chances for success increase when the company representative has planned and prepared for the one analytical at the conference table.

Amiable leaders are pleasant and enjoyable, but are usually reluctant to make a firm decision. They can dodge bullets like no other style. It is very difficult to get amiable leaders to buy off on a new program or idea. In fact, they will resent being pushed toward having to give a yes or no response. Making amiables feel that there is no risk in the decision they are being asked to make is key.

Every career woman should take a style test to gain self-knowledge as well as to learn about personality traits that differ from her own. The two tests that I am most familiar with are Myers-Briggs Type Indicator and Personality Plus. Getting a better understanding of the men managers with whom a woman manager interacts includes learning the weaknesses and strengths of their personality styles.

I Am Woman; Hear Me Roar

I made it a priority to study the men in authority over me in the workplace. As a woman with a very strong style that needs to be continually tempered with graciousness, I have made an observation that has enabled me to function well in a fraternal work environment without compromise to my values:

Strong men rarely know how to manage strong women.

A strong and controlling male manager usually prefers to hire women managers who will accept direction without challenge. Women managers who subject themselves to such working conditions never truly feel empowered. They can easily find themselves functioning as no more than mouthpieces for the strong and controlling male superiors.

The staff who reports to those unempowered women managers will view them as insensitive, out-of-touch with their issues, and unreasonable in their requests. The woman manager who settles for working under unempowered circumstances will earn a reputation as a woman who simply does what she is asked to do and doesn't think for herself, a reputation that can stop her upward progression on the career ladder.

Sometimes a strong and controlling male manager finds that he has ended up with a strong woman manager who reports to him due to circumstances that he did not control, perhaps as a result of his promotion to a new position. This is a very difficult scenario for both the male manager and the woman manager. They are likely to have a relationship of friction. Conflict management can be a good thing, but not when it is between a strong male boss and a strong female who reports to him. The best way to manage a controlling boss is to remember the bottom line that controlling managers seek:

Results, Not Efforts

When a strong woman manager delivers results and meets her commitments, the clash of styles is minimized.

Establishing Rules of Engagement

A new controlling-style leader had inherited me as part of his staff. I wasn't like the male members he was used to having on his staff, neither in thinking process nor in behavior. During his first few weeks I discovered that our management styles and approaches were not simply different; they were diametrically opposed.

During his first attempts to figure out how to approach me, he tried using "you're a sweetheart" to affirm me in passing and in his first staff meeting. A gracious but direct private discussion between the two of us helped him to understand why "sweetheart" was an inappropriate business title for a female manager. He then asked me several times to help him pick out shirts for himself from a clothing catalog. I felt like he was attempting to deal with me as he would with his wife. He also seemed uncomfortable when just the two of us were required to have a private business discussion. He soon began distancing himself from me. It was both amusing and mind-boggling to see a seasoned executive who was so obviously uncomfortable with having a woman on his staff. It was apparent that if I wanted to remain on his staff, I needed to find a way for us to have a business relationship that met him on his turf.

I have found that when men leaders are uncomfortable relating to a woman in a business setting, they revert to how they normally interact with women in social situations. I studied this particular man carefully so that I could understand how I could manage my reactions to his actions. When I met his wife, sure enough he used the "you're a sweetheart" phrase when speaking with her. In his case, his method of communicating with his wife was his interaction comfort zone.

I also researched his work history at previous companies. I learned that his interactions with women employees were primarily with women at the secretarial level. The few women who held lower- to middle-level management positions at his previous companies had tactical responsibilities. He had no experience in managing women who were charged with strategic responsibilities. Armed with this knowledge I knew it would take time and effort on my part to frame our working relationship.

To set our relationship foundation, I contacted former employees of his for topics that were important to him. He loved baseball, so I kept up with current baseball events and discussed them with him. We were both members of the same political party, so we talked politics. My intent was to make him feel more relaxed about working with a woman executive. My goal was to treat him like I would treat a customer.

Our relationship was never one that I would call "warm," but we established the terms by which we could operate. He sought my advice on employee issues and customer relationships. I ended up serving him in a second management position before he moved on. If I hadn't studied him and approached him as I would a customer, the signs were there that my time as part of his staff would have been very short.

How We Confuse Our Male Colleagues

That new company leader's confusion as to how to interact with me was because of his inexperience in dealing with female staff members. There are times, however, when it is the behaviors of women in leadership positions that cause men to become confused, and rightly so. When male managers become confused by a woman manager's actions they will speak poorly about her and will focus on those confusing factors despite all the great things she may be doing.

Men in general have a wonderful ability to aggressively express disagreement on an issue, come to consensus on how the issue will be handled, verbally shake hands and then move on. The complaint I have heard most often from men in authority positions is that women managers tend to rehash past issues that have been long since settled. I can't disagree. It has been my experience as well that many women managers tend to harbor bad feelings towards those who have aggressively debated with them on an issue. Men managers are confused that women managers tend to bring up the same issue over and over again, even after they have agreed to a consensus solution and settled the issue.

Men are increasingly more aware of the need to eliminate sexually harassing behavior. Men become very confused when a woman passes on an email that contains an off-color joke or cartoon, but then expresses that she is highly offended when a joke told in a group setting has a punch line with a double meaning.

Men become confused when women leaders are not consistent in giving direction. I know of a women manager in a Fortune 500 company who supervises a team of primarily male managers. She has developed a reputation as one who gives firm direction on a project, only to change direction with each program review. Her team is slow to complete projects, due to the constant adjustment of direction. Those under her direction often become frustrated and resentful because they know that she'll just change her mind again. Her peers as well as those who work for her speak of her as being wishy-washy, a term that brings the kiss of death to the upwardly mobile female manager.

Men become confused when we unload deep personal details. When a male manager asks a female manager in passing, "How's it going?" he really wants to hear a succinct answer like, "Fine, thanks, how about you?" We confuse men when we respond with great detail about our husband's symptoms when he came down with the flu last week and the specifics of the mouth sore that he developed as a result of the medicine. Our male peer just wants to know what time it is; he doesn't want to know how the watch is built.

Getting Personal

Interaction with women managers on a personal level is especially difficult for the men in authority over us. I worked for a company president who took me to lunch at the beginning of our working relationship so that he could get to know me. In the hour and a half that we spent together he asked for only three basic factual pieces of information: my husband's name and place of employment, our son's name and place of employment, and what kind of car I drove. He never inquired about what I did outside of work or my likes and dislikes.

However, I used the time we spent together at that lunch to ask lots of open-ended questions and learned important information about him. I learned things that helped me to know how to approach him, what was important to him, and what drove him crazy, as well as getting the lowdown on his family. He turned out to be a tough manager, but I had learned how best to approach him, making a challenging relationship much easier and much more successful.

The Sensitive Side

Men become confused when women in authority don't acknowledge their feelings when they make themselves vulnerable. I came to realize this through an incident that involved one of the most talented men that I ever mentored. I was his manager at the time, and he was complaining to me about the hard time he was having on an assigned project, how long it was taking him, and all the obstacles he was facing. Instead of acknowledging his pain, I tersely said, "Just get it done!"

He was shocked and confused by my insensitive response and shut down for three days. I went to him to get him to open back up, and our discussion sensitized me to the fact that big, strong, confident-appearing guys have feelings, too. As a result, from that time forward, and despite periodically being called "Momma Pam" by a certain male manager who is near and dear to my heart, I made myself available to male managers who needed to vent to someone who could "feel their pain." Bosses vented, peers vented, subordinates vented; I empathized and advised. Each time, the benefit for me was a deeper understanding of the male colleague customer with whom I was interacting, which yielded an improved working relationship.

The Hard Cases

There will always be customers of a business who are totally unreasonable and even irrational. They seem to delight in abusive behavior. In the same way, women managers will encounter male manager customers who have terrible tempers and short fuses. These male manager customers need to be studied from a safe distance.

Perhaps these male customers perceive that the stronger they come across, the more results they seem to get. Getting to know them better is not a possibility because they lock everyone out, especially a female manager. But there may be a key in there somewhere that might reveal itself as they are studied.

A business can make a decision to discontinue interaction with customers who are just too aggravating. Unfortunately, women managers can't simply decide to ignore difficult male leaders who are part of the management team. Self-control becomes the solution. The Guidebook states it simply:

> *A fool gives full vent to his anger,*
> *but a wise man keeps himself under control.*
> *—Proverbs 29:11*

If a woman responds to a male colleague's fit of anger by exhibiting angry behavior herself, there are now two fools in the room. A woman cannot control the actions of a man who freely vents his anger, but she has power over the situation when she uses self-control as her response.

I worked for one executive who vented his anger by throwing whatever was in his hand at the time. His style included trying to intimidate those on his staff by verbally exploding using strong profanity. By studying him, I could see that the most violent explosions took place in large groups. He never vented his anger in front of me in a one-on-one situation, and rarely in small group meetings. One obvious way to manage him was to have meetings with him which limited the number of attendees to four whenever possible. For those times when a group meeting was required and he brought out the anger, the only wise way to react was to stay under control until he settled down and spoke rationally.

Onward and Upward

Women who strategically study the men with whom they interact will equip themselves with the adeptness needed to successfully maneuver among the men colleagues they encounter on their career paths. A woman who chooses not to treat men as customers will find herself repeatedly stepping down from career ladders, only to move over to a different ladder where she'll likely find a whole new group of men customers who need to be studied.

The better decision is for a woman to plant her feet firmly on her ladder of choice, and to reach for the next rung by studying men colleagues carefully, using information and observations as valuable tools to manage her actions and reactions for success.

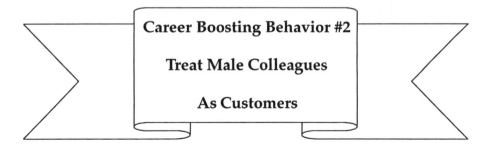

Career Boosting Behavior #2

Treat Male Colleagues

As Customers

SABOTAGE #3

Key Concepts

- Mentors facilitate promotions, advancement and achievement
- Mentors should change as circumstances change
- Mentors influence the decision-maker in hiring and promotion choices

Sabotage #3

Failing to Find a Mentor

The Value of Mentors

The origin of the word *mentor* appears to be a character in Homer's epic, *The Odyssey*. Mentor was a teacher who guided the hero's son. Today's business use of the term *mentor* describes an experienced colleague who makes him or herself available to advise and encourage others.

How does a woman learn to handle experiences that she hasn't had yet? Courses on business techniques are important and books on leadership topics are useful, but the value of bouncing specific business challenges and new ideas off successful leadership role models is priceless. Making mistakes through personal experience can be an effective teaching method, but a less painful route is one that benefits from somebody else's trials and errors.

I never would have advanced in my career to the extent that I did without the mentors that were a part of my success. Having a mentor is a key career goal asset, one that has a profound effect in providing opportunities for advancement up the corporate ladder.

Hitching Your Wagon

A CEO friend of my husband's has always had women managers in key positions on his staff. He values the unique qualities that women managers bring to a team. He invests time mentoring women, and in return he has a team that works to insure *his* success.

I think there are several reasons why a man in a leadership position would invest in developing women managers. He may get a bit of an ego boost in having a hand in the success of someone against whom the odds of moving up are stacked. There are also bragging rights associated with a skill that finds diamonds in the rough and develops them into successful women leaders. But, above all it is an incredibly bright move for a male manager to understand his weaknesses and balance them with the strengths of women leaders who are wired differently.

There was an absence of successful women executives and upper level managers in the career path I chose to take. In fact, I had neither a direct nor an indirect reporting relationship to a female manager at any point in my career. Consequently, all of my mentors were men. All of them were great leadership examples who possessed specific strengths that I needed to develop within myself. Most—but not all— of my mentors started out as my direct manager.

From time to time, I found that I needed to add new mentors to my career support team. When a mentor would leave the company I replaced him with someone else within the organization. A mentor's departure repositions him or her from an internal mentor to an external mentor. External mentors provide great value when a manager needs to bounce an idea off a respected colleague who has no vested interest in the outcome. They can give input from a completely neutral position and more importantly they possess a much broader range of vision that extends beyond the limitations of a company's boundaries.

As I progressed up the ladder my mentoring needs evolved. Sometimes it was necessary to seek out a new mentor who had skills and experience that matched new challenges I was facing. I believe that each woman in management should have about a half dozen mentor/ advisors with varying skills and experience on her support team.

How to Get the Boss's Job

My first mentor was affectionately known as the office curmudgeon. He was *tough*. By being tough, he taught me the no-holds-barred basics of the business and how to prosper in it. If I asked him if he had heard of a certain product, his retort was, "Did you look in your catalog?" If I hadn't, and it was in there, heaven help me. I'd get a lecture on one of several topics that ranged from "don't depend on others to do my work for me" to "how did I ever expect to advance in the company if I didn't know what the company sold." There were no shortcuts permitted. However, if I had a legitimate need, he was the first one to get on my team to facilitate getting the job done. It was his hard-line training that enabled me to take my first step into management. Several years later, I was promoted into his position.

My mentor during my sales management development was on the company fast track. Though we started as peers, I came to directly report to him as he took a giant and well-deserved leap up the ladder. He stretched me like a rubber band. I could never get results fast enough. He pushed me to achieve all the while he affirmed his faith in me. As challenging as it was to work for him, I was energized by his style. After a couple of years, I was promoted into the management position that he had held when he first mentored me.

My favorite mentor is still mentoring me. We began our relationship when the president of a company handpicked me for a new position and recommended me to the new executive head of a department. The executive not only promoted me into the position, but he also took me under his wing and invested in me to the fullest. I was challenged to perform at a whole new level of excellence. He taught me a new set of globally transferable skills that some years later enabled me to achieve a senior staff position—the very position he had held when we began our mentor-mentee relationship.

This particular mentor influenced most of my significant middle-management career decisions. We had and continue to have a great trust relationship. He once asked me to accept a director level position that would require me to lead an area that included a business segment in which I had little experience. Although I knew how to manage product lines, I had done very little with product design. He addressed my weakness head on, and committed to helping me make it a strength. His words that influenced me the most in accepting the position were these: "You know I'd never encourage you to step into a position that I knew you couldn't handle." Because of our trust relationship, I did indeed know that and accepted the offer.

Advice from the Guidebook

Women who feel that they can achieve great accomplishments on their own without help will watch their careers fold in on them. Every career woman needs trustworthy advisors who can lend different perspectives on issues and opportunities. The Guidebook puts it succinctly:

Plans fail for lack of counsel, but with many advisers they succeed.
—*Proverbs 15:22*

I remember the kudos I received from a corporate president who was part of the senior management group to whom I was pitching a new program. He said, "This is a great plan. Who did you run this past that helped you bring it to this level?" My next overhead slide listed the names and titles of the industry advisors. He smiled and said, "It was clear that you didn't do this in a vacuum. Well done."

Until I received that affirmation, I had thought that my solicitation of industry leader input for the program might be viewed as a weakness by the corporate president. I was actually going to hold the overhead slide back, anticipating a response of "What's the matter? Can't you think of a program on your own?" His positive reaction helped me to realize that he probably had his own set of advisers and mentors who contributed to *his* success.

When I made the decision to start a small business, I sought out the advice of business people whose accomplishments I admired. In addition to my favorite mentor, I selected a woman who had opened and closed several businesses and who was embarking on a new speaking career. I used the services of a career transition counselor and met with a marketing specialist that the career facilitator recommended.

A key set of advisors was a husband and wife team who had founded a ten million-dollar high-tech business. When I started an organization for women in management, I asked this particular advisor team to review and critique my web site before it hit the public. Having a support team of experienced mentors was invaluable in facilitating a successful transition from working for a corporation into becoming a business owner.

The Guidebook highlights the "no pain, no gain" aspect of a mentoring relationship:

As iron sharpens iron, so one man sharpens another.
—*Proverbs 27:17*

When a piece of iron is used to shape another piece of iron, a honing process takes place in which sharpness is produced by filing away particles of the iron. Sometimes sparks fly during the process. In the same manner, a mentoring relationship may involve some disagreements. Each person in the relationship will sharpen the other as different points of view are presented.

Some mentoring advice will be difficult to swallow. My favorite mentor wanted to include one of his own advisors in a planned luncheon we were having together. I objected. I had some private issues that I needed to discuss and I didn't care to have a third party hear the details. My mentor wisely let the idea simmer for two weeks, and then brought it up again. This time, he said, "It will be good for you to get another perspective on the main issue that you and I plan to discuss. You and I can continue privately after lunch on the other issues that I know you want to keep between us."

I reluctantly agreed to a shared lunch opportunity. To my surprise, I benefited from advice given by the third party advisor, and to my even greater surprise, I learned that several years back he had directed my selection from a pool of middle-management talent for a key position. This lunch event reminded me that my role as the "mentee" in the mentoring relationship is to be open to the recommendations and advice of the mentor.

Three Guys in the Guidebook

A perfect Guidebook example of a mentoring relationship is that of two colleagues named Paul and Timothy. Paul had the greater life experience and served as Timothy's mentor. The two colleagues had established a trust relationship in which Timothy knew that Paul not only led by example, but also had his best interests at heart. Timothy had great respect for Paul's counsel.

In the same manner, a woman's business mentors need to be leaders whom she respects for their accomplishments and with whom she can establish a trust relationship. Successful women have one or more persons like Paul in their work life at all times, and they choose them wisely.

Another mentoring relationship mentioned in the Guidebook is that of Paul and Barnabas. Barnabas worked with Paul as a peer and served as Paul's encourager. The mentor that I previously referred to as my favorite mentor has transitioned into the role of a person like Barnabas. This mentor and I still get together for dinner to celebrate both our birthdays. When I began entertaining the idea of starting a business, he was at the top of my list of advisors to call because of the encouraging role he has played in my life.

Getting Your Ticket Punched

Each step up the career ladder depends on someone making a hiring or promotion decision that sanctions the advancement. Most of the time there is also another person in the process who influences or facilitates the decision. Somebody has to "punch your ticket." In each of my significant management career steps—hourly employee to supervisor, supervisor to manager, manager to director, and director to vice president—it was my mentor at that time who either personally punched the ticket, or who significantly influenced the person who made the decision.

My opportunity to move into senior management came when the company where I directed the activities of a large sales team decided to split into two separate companies. The vice president of sales, who was one of my mentors, accepted a promotion to the corporate level. His career move opened up a vice president of sales position at each of the two split companies.

I knew I would be a great fit for the opening at the company where the challenge would be the greatest. I made an appointment with the combined company president so that I could ask for the job. Prior to my scheduled meeting my mentor, knowing of my desire to land the position, spoke to the president about my abilities. During the meeting, I asked for the opportunity to make the career move. The president looked at me and said, "You know what? I'm going to bet on you" and gave me the job. While he punched the actual ticket, I have no doubt that the influence of my promoted mentor played a part in the president's decision. Not to minimize the importance of a woman's own abilities in any way, but it certainly helps to have a supporter or supporters greasing the wheel on your behalf.

When one of my friends who was a young and aggressive corporate-level vice-president felt that he was ready to be president of a company, he found it impossible to step up to that rung. No one wanted to fill the top position of a company with someone who had no previous experience as a company president. His mentor at the time, a group president, offered him the position of company president for one of the companies in his division. That was the good news. The bad news was the location of the company: it was in a cold and remote area of the country where the excitement of the day was watching wild turkeys cross the road.

His mentor told him straight out that he needed his ticket punched and assured my friend that if he would tough it out for a year, he would be playing on a new level-one where he would have more offers for president level positions than he could handle. My friend accepted the job. Within just a few months, ahead of his mentor's prediction, my friend moved on to a bigger and better opportunity as president of a company that was located in a warm climate and that offered him the pressure-cooker environment in which he thrived. He trusted his mentor and it paid off.

As a Bonus . . .

In addition to the advice and encouragement that mentors provide there is a bonus. Mentors make great references when on the job hunt. Who knows your value better than they do? Adding mentors to your career armamentarium is a strategic move that facilitates the ability to advance. Just as tutors improve scholastic results and coaches raise athletic ability and self-esteem, mentors facilitate career achievement.

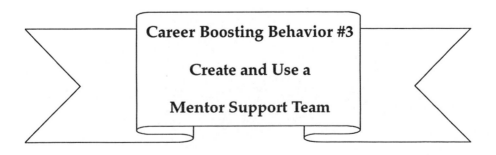

Career Boosting Behavior #3

Create and Use a

Mentor Support Team

SABOTAGE #4

Key Concepts

- A woman influences more people than she thinks she does
- Influence can be positive or negative
- Mentoring others improves personal effectiveness

SABOTAGE #4

Underestimating Your Influence on Others

The World Is Watching

In my early days as a marketing manager, I received a great gift from one of the company's vice-presidents when he asked me a question. During a one-on-one discussion with him about a situation that was only peripherally related to my position, I told him I was curious as to why he wanted my opinion. He looked at me with a smile, and said, "You really have no idea just how many people you influence, do you?"

I remember being stunned as he unfolded just a few of the ways that employees and managers in various company locations had handled situations based on my suggestions. I actually felt burdened by the thought that people were taking action on comments into which I had put very little thought. Thanks to that senior manager who took a few mentor moments to enlighten me, I gained a heightened understanding of the responsibility that comes with being in a position of leadership.

Once a woman understands and embraces the concept that she influences more people than she thinks she does, and in more ways than she ever imagined, she can use her influence as a powerful success tool.

Tapping the Power Within

The majority of the women that I have known throughout my career have been much better "people managers" than were most of the male managers whose paths I've crossed. Women in management positions are usually quite skilled at developing loyalty from the team assigned to them.

Unfortunately, I have seen too many women managers waste the energy of influence through a "my way or the highway" leadership style. Everything looks like a nail to a woman manager who uses her power like a hammer. A harshly demanding and controlling leadership style stifles employee creativity and undermines the leader's ability to learn from those more closely aligned with the inner workings of the business. A controlling manager sabotages her career by undermining her own support system.

At the other end of the spectrum are women managers who take their leadership influence and simply file it away. They do their jobs well, but they fail to tap into their power by releasing its force. They stop short of pulling out the best that those under their sphere of influence can give. I have watched several women managers limit their own careers because they never mentored anyone. These talented women were passed over for promotional opportunities because they were holding on to their job assignments so tightly that they never developed an heir apparent or two. With no one groomed to take over her position, a woman manager can box herself in and limit her advancement.

Bringing Out the Best

To use the power of influence, a woman needs to become a mentor to others. Women have a natural nurturing ability that enables them to assist others to achieve success. There is immense personal reward when an experienced woman leader sees great potential within someone less experienced and is given the privilege of being an advisor. The best that a mentee has to offer might be hidden under a lot of rough edges. Iron still sharpens iron (Proverbs 27) whether a woman is the mentee or the mentor. Bringing out the best in others brings out the best in the mentor as well.

The successful mentor-mentee relationship depends a great deal on the goals and attitude of the person being mentored. I once hired two college students, one male and one female, for an internship program in which they would share one position, six months at a time. Both had an identical opportunity to demonstrate leadership potential.

The female intern expressed early on that she had her sights set on marriage and a family, and not a career. She dedicated herself to doing the work required of her in the internship so that she could pass her college requirements. At the completion of the internship, she took a clerical position with a company until she could fulfill her dream of marrying and then of having a family. She successfully reached her personal goals.

The male intern, on the other hand, convinced me that he wanted to be mentored to success in a business career. At the completion of the internship, I hired him in a full-time customer support position. We continued the mentoring relationship, and I facilitated his promotion into a sales position. He became an overachiever and was eventually hired by a competitor into his first management position. He continued up the ladder and became a senior vice president with a large corporation.

When he tells the story of his success, he credits two people as being responsible for his climb up the ladder: his father, and me. I could not have invested my time into a more worthy cause. There are few things more rewarding than having someone that you mentored give you the credit for his or her success. The bonus is that I became a better manager through the mentoring relationship.

During my time in sales management, I interviewed a candidate for a sales position who overwhelmed me with his talent and potential. I wanted the opportunity to be responsible for this man's success. It took three "final" interviews with him to convince him that his future would be exceptional if he accepted my offer.

He finally accepted and became the number one sales representative for several years. He earned the respect of his peers and became a mentor himself to many representatives, both novice and seasoned, and moved up into management. We have more of a peer mentoring relationship now and I am still affirming him, eagerly awaiting his next career move.

What's In It for Me?

Many of the women managers I have known have directed the majority of their management efforts toward pleasing the boss. One manager expressed to me that supervisors and managers often feel trapped because they do things that they feel must be done only because the boss wants them done, and not because they believe it's the right move to make. There's no freedom in a narrow management focus that only pleases the boss; there are also few promotional opportunities.

When a woman manager mentors the employees who report to her she finds herself leading a team of highly skilled employees who handle the tactical issues, freeing her to address strategic ones. Strategic thinkers impress bosses; so does a manager who develops an inspired team. When a manager can accomplish both, other executives take note of her demonstrated leadership skills. These other executives can be responsible for new career ladders.

When a woman mentors people who don't report to her, she gains knowledge and perspective on other areas of the company. These relationships increase her ability to plan from a total company view rather than just a departmental view. Gaining allies in other areas of the company also increases her career opportunities.

The relationship between a woman leader and those she mentors yields another important benefit that manifests itself when she pursues a new job opportunity. A potential employer who wants to get a complete picture of an applicant's abilities and skills will not limit the reference check to former bosses. The reference check is likely to include at least one peer relationship, a directly supervised employee or two, and someone over whom she had influence who was not in a reporting relationship. The people that a woman mentors can serve as references who can attest to her leadership skills as well as to her expertise in guiding and developing people.

From the Guidebook

The Guidebook depicts leaders as having responsibility for more than just their own career advancements:

Each of you should look not only to your own interests but also to the interests of others.
—*Philippians 2:4*

A woman who fills the mentor role of Paul, whose relationship with Timothy is mentioned in the previous chapter, arms herself with a valuable success tool that will enhance her reputation as a leader. Smart women leaders seek out people with great potential and invest in their career development. A woman becomes a better manager when she knows that others are depending upon her leadership example as a model for their career behavior.

Self Check

The working world is watching. Younger women are emulating the actions of current women leaders. What do we look like to a watching work society? Will the way we are managing our careers open doors for other women? Will it open doors for us?

To secure her footing on the career ladder of choice and to be the kind of example that less experienced men and women managers need to model, a woman in management needs to do a self-examination by asking this question:

Do my actions align with my career goals?

Every action a woman leader takes will either bring her closer to her career goals or take her farther away from them. If a woman's actions don't reflect her stated goals, she becomes stuck on the same rung of the same ladder for some time to come as the power of her position starts to fade. No one seeks out a mentor who isn't making an impact.

There are some actions that not only fail to align with a woman's career goals, but also cause her to lose her footing at the top of a long chute, often taking a few other women down the slide with her. Unprofessional behavior by a woman in a leadership position adversely influences her own career path as well as the career opportunities for other women in her organization.

The Power of Influence

A woman's power to influence manifests itself in one of three forms: untapped and dormant, negatively impacting others through substandard performance, or flourishing in her role as a mentor. Every woman gets to make her own choice as to what she'll do with her power. Successful women will use their role of authority to influence and develop others.

The true measure of a woman's leadership lies in
the well being and quality of those she leads.

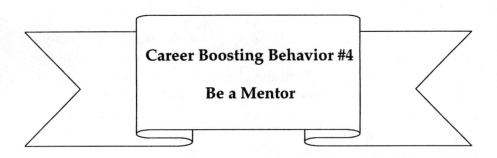

Career Boosting Behavior #4

Be a Mentor

SABOTAGE #5

Key Concepts

- A woman's behavior can deface her desired image
- Self-control facilitates career advancement
- Moderation facilitates self-control

SABOTAGE #5

Vandalizing Your Image

Image Can Be Injured

A woman who renovates her home to achieve a desired image would never purposely vandalize it. Yet women choose to vandalize their professional images through behavior that is inappropriate for a woman in a leadership position. Behavior that defaces a woman's image can leave irreparable career damage.

I admired a particular female executive's style. She dressed in office attire that was distinctly feminine but mindfully professional. She was an excellent communicator and had developed an exemplary reputation throughout the organization.

But her decision to let loose at the company Christmas party is one I'll never forget. All heads turned as she entered wearing a revealing sequined dress, slit to midthigh level. She frequented the open bar during the party, and although her husband was with her, she pretty much danced with everybody but him. As she pulled a senior executive out onto the dance floor, I saw darts shoot out from the eyes of the executive's wife. As a result of letting loose at an office party, she became the hot office gossip topic for months. The management team viewed her differently from that point on; she had vandalized her image.

There are two opposing ways to become the talk of the company:
by achieving exceptional results, or by letting your hair down
at a company event.

To Drink, or Not to Drink

Work events that take place after business hours often involve alcohol. If a woman wants to protect her image, alcohol consumption at Christmas parties, cocktail parties, and client dinners needs to be managed.

From time to time the health benefits of drinking a glass of wine at night are touted on the evening news. Interestingly enough, the proper use of wine in ancient times was indeed for health benefit. Even the Guidebook illustrates the medicinal value of alcohol in the instruction to "stop drinking only water, and use a little wine because of your stomach and your frequent illness."

Notice that the instruction states "a little" wine, not "a lot" of wine. The Guidebook advocates moderate behavior. Leaders in general are cautioned against "indulging in much wine" and women in particular who are serving as leadership examples are instructed not to be "addicted to much wine." The Guidebook also gives a good visual in presenting why the overuse of wine and beer should be avoided:

> *Wine is a mocker and beer a brawler;*
> *whoever is led astray by them is not wise.*
> —*Proverbs 20:1*

Hollywood presents us with a fairly accurate picture of beer brawls, except that on the big screen, everybody seems to recover without serious injury. Comedians mock drunks in their comedy routines while the audience howls with laughter at their foolish appearance. Likewise, a woman who chooses to become inebriated at company events will look foolish to those who witness her behavior. She also may say or do things that she will regret later.

Women who have had too much to drink make careless decisions and become neglectful in managing themselves and their personal items. A woman manager friend on a business trip had her purse hanging on the back of a barstool while she had a few drinks and a few laughs. A stranger scooped up her purse strap as he passed behind her and quickly left the bar. By the time another bar patron was able to alert her, the man was long gone. My friend spent most of the night on the telephone making special arrangements to be able to board a plane since she was midway through a business trip and now had no identification. She lost quite a bit of money, her license, passport, and credit cards, and she put the remainder of the business trip in jeopardy.

Preventative Measures

Moderation is good wisdom to use in just about every situation—in the use of alcohol, as well as for work and life strategies in general. Moderation means discretion, restraint, and self-control. Wine aficionados who know and enjoy excellent wine savor it and drink it with great intent. They carefully taste the wine, searching out its unique characteristics and then pair it with appropriate foods. They don't guzzle down glass after glass to see how much of the good wine they can drink before last call.

If self-control is an issue for a woman when it comes to drinking, the one and only way to prevent an embarrassing or harmful experience at the hands of alcohol is not to have alcohol at all. I know managers who carry a glass of ginger ale on ice to help them feel less conspicuous when mingling at company events. They not only blend in, but they have an added bonus of avoiding the lip-loosening affects of alcohol.

If a woman is participating in a reception before a business dinner and would enjoy gently sipping a glass of wine, that is her privilege. But, since the best wine is usually selected for dinner, why waste calories on reception wine that is usually just the house brand? If she passes on the white zinfandel; she'll find that it's worth the wait for a carefully selected wine at dinner.

Men and Their Alcohol Moments

When men have their alcohol moments, they can create unpleasant and even dangerous situations for female colleagues. A male consultant hired by the company where I worked at the time had a reputation for becoming an angry drunk. He attended a company-sponsored reception at a hotel where the guests were important female customers, both supervisors and managers. As per reputation, he became intoxicated, began loudly using four letters words, offended many of the customers, and became belligerent when asked to leave. Before he could be successfully removed from the room, he stumbled into the bathroom and set a towel on fire with his carelessly tossed cigarette. As the result of his alcohol moment, the company needed to initiate an aggressive relationship repair process with several important customers who had witnessed his behavior.

I attended a business meeting where a male manager began drinking margaritas upon arriving at the company-sponsored cocktail hour. He downed several large glasses in a row and passed out in front of his peers and subordinates. Just before he passed out, he babbled incoherently as he draped himself across the lap of a shocked female manager. The woman manager had to be rescued by others in attendance when she couldn't move his dead weight off her legs. During the three-day business meeting which followed the opening party, attendees distanced themselves from him. His credibility had been compromised and the participants paid little attention to his presentations.

At one time, I reported to a newly promoted department head. At his first company meeting as upper management, he arrived early to the evening cocktail party and began drinking. After a few hours had passed, I entered the room. He came to me with a beer bottle in his hand and asked me to step outside into the hallway to discuss a work issue.

As he spoke to me he slurred his words. He was inebriated and had to steady himself by placing his hand against the hallway wall. He proceeded to tell me that he had been attracted to me ever since the first time we had worked together. I told him that he needed to go back to his hotel room and get some rest. I then left the area. I was told that after I had removed myself from the situation he returned to the party and continued drinking to a point where no one could understand his words. When he attempted to toss an empty bottle into the trash, the poorly thrown bottle hit the wall instead, shattering glass in all directions.

The next day he had a major headache and no recollection of his words to me. He profusely apologized for his actions when I told him what he had said. Since I had not felt that I was in physical danger, I decided to address the issue with him and consider it as an isolated incident. However, I did a "note to file" which captured the date of the event, time, the conversation, and others at the event who had seen him in that condition in case there should be a similar incident in the future. As a result of this event, I counsel other women that if there is even a hint of a dangerous or inappropriate situation with a male who's had too much to drink, she should immediately remove herself from the area without apology and document the details.

And Women and Theirs

A woman will find it difficult to have self-control when she's put hefty amounts of alcohol into her body. By far, the majority of the stories that I have heard repeated about the embarrassing moments of women leaders involve excessive use of alcohol.

Every company has an embarrassing incident that stands out from the others. A former company's story that topped the list is known as the "Hot Tub Incident." A very talented woman joined the company in her first management position. She came with an educational and professional background that gave her instant credibility. She was extremely knowledgeable and had great people interaction skills. There was early talk of a promising company career track. And then came her first sales meeting.

Sales meetings are times of great celebration. Sales achievers are honored. Great camaraderie develops among members of the sales team and the management team. The meetings provide a relaxed atmosphere that facilitates interaction. However, when massive quantities of alcohol are added to the mix, the interaction can take a hazardous turn.

The new woman manager's vibrant personality and excellent training won over the crowd during the meeting. Exuberant after a successful three-day event, she decided to spend the last evening mixing with the sales team in the hospitality suite where liquor lined the room and where many admired a large Jacuzzi tub in the suite's bathroom.

I was in charge of locking down the suite at midnight. The party was still in full swing when I arrived and I could hear the Jacuzzi jets at full force. When I opened the door to the bathroom, there was the new woman manager sitting in the Jacuzzi clothed only in her bra and pantyhose. Next to her in the tub sat a male member of the sales team, in the buff. It was obvious by her giggles that she had consumed more than her fair share of alcohol.

I attempted to get her out of the tub. She wouldn't budge. I shuffled everybody else out of the suite and finally talked her into going to bed. I made sure she was up and showered the next morning so that she was present and accounted for at the new president's closing address.

Unfortunately, too many people had witnessed the Jacuzzi incident. The gossip spread like wildfire and eventually reached the ears of the new president. As a result, the tub story replaced the talk of a promising career. She not only slid down that large chute, she left the company and stepped back into a non-management role. It was truly a career-ending moment.

Having an Affair

Women managers can make bad choices that are not connected to alcohol. Having an office affair is one of them. It can happen to anyone, even to women who feel completely in control and who are without a thought in that direction. It starts with a flirtatious comment and takes off from there. The phrase "innocent flirting" is an oxymoron. Flirting leads you farther into temptation than you even intend to go. Flirting is never innocent; it is always intentional.

All women who want to keep their feet firmly planted on the success ladder when it comes to office relationships with the opposite sex need to remember this phrase:

Stay dressed for success.

What follows is a small sampling of a few career women in management who didn't stay dressed and the impact it had on their careers:

The married department manager of a company where I was employed worked a great deal of overtime with his female department supervisor. When a member of the cleaning staff opened the door to the ladies room one night, she found the two of them engaged in a sexual act right there on the sofa. The result of the incident was that both managers were fired.

A woman making her first move to management began an office affair with another manager. Her husband discovered their liaison when he came home early, picked up the phone extension, and overheard an intimate conversation. She chose to leave the company to save her marriage and took a lesser paying position in order to make the move quickly.

A former leader of a company where I worked was going through a messy divorce. Over a period of about a month, he asked various female managers to go to dinner with him where there would be no talk about work. Most declined; one married woman manager did not. Shortly after the dinner, she entered into an on-going affair with him, which often took place on company time. One day she asked a female manager friend to cover for her while she met him at a hotel. As a result of this request, the friendship between those two women was damaged. The affair ran its course and the married female manager left the company.

After the affair ended, this same leader hired a female to fill an upper management position. They, too, began an affair that encroached on company time. The company owners received evidence of the liaison and fired both of them on the same day.

The bottom line: Nobody wins in an office affair.

Be Beyond Reproach

The Guidebook advises leaders who want to avoid sliding down the chute that leads to the gossip mill to be "beyond reproach." To be beyond reproach means to have a reputation that includes prudent management of behaviors while on the job, both during normal business hours and after work. A woman who is beyond reproach thinks through situations to ensure that her actions will not harm or vandalize her reputation and career.

Women need to keep the idea of being beyond reproach in front of them in the way they dress. A woman's choice of dress should be for success, not seduction. When I travel on business, I wear conservative business outfits (jacket, pants, and white blouse; or jacket, below-the-knee-length-skirt, and white blouse) in large part because it prevents the exposure of skin that I'm not interested in having a male counterpart see. The bonus to beyond-reproach dressing is that is makes for easy mixing and matching of outfits, so there is less luggage to manage.

When I led the sales department of a company, I sometimes had no option but to use my hotel room to conduct interviews of applicants for sales positions. Whenever possible, I chose a small suite where the sleeping portion of the room could be closed off from the meeting area. If a room with a Murphy bed (a bed that folds up into the wall) was available, I'd make arrangements for the hotel staff to fold the bed into the wall early in the morning while I was at breakfast, and bring in a table with two chairs. Hotels were always willing to comply.

If my only option was a sleeping room with round table and chairs, I would prop the door slightly open during the interview. If the room had a heavy metal hinged intruder lock, I would swing it over and use it to hold the door open. I didn't mind at all when hotel security would see the slightly open door and would double-check to make certain that all was well. Being beyond reproach extends to behavior that protects your personal safety as well as your reputation.

Hold Yourself Accountable

Planning for success in social interaction with business colleagues is just as important as planning for success in daily projects. A woman's most powerful tool for remaining beyond reproach is self-accountability. I found it effective to picture someone who would cause me to feel uncomfortable if that person were to be next to me watching me doing something dishonorable. A woman can manage her behaviors by taking a quick self-test before taking action:

> Would I feel good about doing this if my husband
> (son, daughter, mentor, pastor) were standing beside me?

If the answer to the test is "no," the response is simple. Don't do it.

Asset Management

From the Guidebook:

> In everything set them an example by doing what is good.
> In your teaching show integrity, seriousness and soundness
> of speech that cannot be condemned, so that those who oppose
> you may be ashamed because they have nothing bad to say . . . .
> —Titus 2:7-8

The achievement and maintenance of a reputation that includes morality and self-control is one of the most precious and priceless assets that a career woman can possess. It minimizes the amount of self-imposed time that she spends floating around in the gossip pool. Alcohol users need to practice moderation and romance seekers need to look outside the office in order to prevent image injury.

Choosing prudent behavior facilitates a woman manager's upward career motion by giving her a firm grasp on her career ladder while she stretches for the next rung.

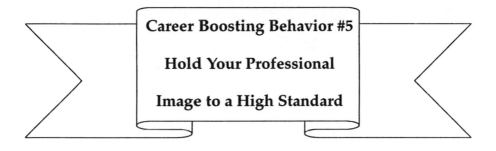

Career Boosting Behavior #5

Hold Your Professional

Image to a High Standard

SABOTAGE #6

Key Concepts

- Negativity self-limits achievement
- Chaos creates opportunity
- A woman has a choice in how to respond to negative events

SABOTAGE #6

Whining Instead of Shining

No Whine During Work Hours

At times, both men and women leaders complain about work events. There is a difference, though, in the labels that are normally used for describing a complaining male manager versus those used for a complaining female manager.

I have heard male leaders carry on in a way that absolutely deserved a retort of "stop whining." However, men have done a good job in claiming positive-sounding descriptive synonyms that portray strength such as "protest," "gripe," "snarl," and "not going down without a fight." The words used by male managers when describing female managers are generally negative-sounding verbs that carry an emotionally weak context such as "fuss," "pitch a fit," "whimper," "cry," "pout," and chief among their descriptive terms, "whine."

Women might not like being labeled as whiners when they voice complaints, but the business world supports it. Since we've been given the full rights of ownership to the word "whining," it needs to be, at best, banished thorough counter-supportive behavior or, at very least, managed well.

A woman will never achieve her professional
goals if she is tagged with a reputation as a whiner.

Whining Is Self-Limiting

I worked with a woman manager who earned her reputation as a whiner. It seemed as though she made it a daily goal to look for things over which to complain. She had a talent for turning lunch conversation with her peers into a groan-and-moan session. If another manager excelled and was rewarded for good work, she grumbled that it was favoritism. When a female peer was promoted to be her supervisor, she pouted in meetings and clearly indicated her displeasure with the new reporting relationship.

She frequently protested that she was not being promoted and blamed the company for her lack of advancement. Sadly, it was her own negative mindset that limited her ability to achieve. Her negative thinking even blocked her creativity. She made it known that much of her work came from the output of other managers who had previously worked in the same department. Over time she developed a reputation for tweaking existing documents and claiming them as her own.

It was frustrating for me to see this women manager choose to fail by selecting whining over shining. Her résumé demonstrated a logical career progression and she was well educated with a completed master's degree. While she expressed a desire to move up on the company ladder and to use her education to the fullest, she did little to actually make it happen.

When the company began to downsize, she found herself as one of many managers being interviewed for half as many available positions. She was not a successful candidate. The managers chosen, both male and female, were selected in great part due to their reputations as creative, positive thinkers who had demonstrated constructive results.

No-Whining Zone

Gaining and maintaining a positive attitude falls under a principle that I call the "put on, put off" life rule. The more you do a positive activity, the less you do a negative activity. The more you feed on positive thoughts, the less room you have for negative thoughts. Having fewer negative thoughts yields less whining and complaining.

The rubber meets the road when crisis events enter the work arena. The budget is significantly cut; the company puts a freeze on new hires just before two of your key employees resign; rumors of a lay-off permeate the premises. Such events are fodder for whiners.

When rumors of a huge downsizing proved true and eliminated the management position I held at that time, my husband posted a sign on my bedroom bureau which read:

Lemonade for Sale

That sign served as a great reminder to me that I should not stop at just making lemonade from the lemon I was handed; I needed to get right back out there and sell that lemonade. Choosing to sit around and whine about a job loss gains nothing.

A company downsizing is business. It's not personal. And, even if a woman believes with her whole heart that the root cause was a personal bias or vendetta, it's still just business. If she views it any other way, she'll become a whiner, not a shiner.

For Those Who Remain

Anyone who has been through a significant company downsizing knows that the people who remain after the cut are asked to do much more work at the same or even less compensation. It can be frustrating and highly stressful, especially for managers when they and their teams are crushed with additional tasks. If a woman is working from a negative mindset, the chaos of the aftermath will overwhelm her. Her leadership will reflect a resentful attitude. Those under her direction will emulate her, and she'll soon drive her team into the ground.

My all-time favorite customer service manager was recently called on to lead her team in the aftermath of a layoff that eliminated 15% of the company employees at all levels. Her choice on how to react was before her: whine or shine?

She chose to shine. She led her team through months of chaotic dark times. She managed with her usual care and concern for each employee. Despite her best efforts, several key people jumped ship. She didn't lose heart; she continued to do the best that she could for the customers with the limited resources that she had remaining. While she had no choice in her circumstances, her reaction to those circumstances was completely in her control. She chose wisely.

Only those managers who lead from a well-entrenched positive mindset will have the vision to see the chaos in terms of what it really does:

Chaos creates opportunity.

Careers have been launched as the result of chaotic circumstances. The chaos that was created by one company's downsizing facilitated two significant career advancements in the same department. A junior-level line manager became a full-fledged department manager, and a director moved up into her first vice president role when an executive-level manager buckled under the pressure of the post-layoff environment and resigned.

When a woman focuses on the negative,
she misses the opportunity to step up and shine.

The Daily Grind

Keeping a positive attitude in the face of a significant event such as a downsizing can actually be easier than staying positive when facing year after year of difficult daily struggles with one small crisis after another. This constant pressure can be draining. However, as long as a manager chooses to receive a paycheck from an organization, the manager is accountable for demonstrating consistent and positive attitude and leadership.

In my experience, when the daily stress level within a company escalates off the chart, male managers tend to move on to another company. Women managers tend to stick it out. If in sticking it out, the woman manager watches for opportunities that inevitably come from chaotic situations, she may be poised for a positive career move.

Unfortunately, company-loyal women can become overwhelmed by the negative circumstances and react with negative leadership. Their physical health begins to show the signs of stress. Negative comments infect those on the teams they lead and it isn't long before complaining and whining about the situation becomes the norm for the whole department.

You Can't Be Sad and Stay

There are times when women managers need to consider that their behavior indicates that a career change might be best for them. When all attempts fail in helping a manager or an employee to embrace a positive attitude, I use a little decision grid to help put the situation into perspective:

PS	PL
NL	NS

Figure 1

There are four boxes on the decision grid (Figure 1). Three out of four of these are decision options that are available to each manager and each employee. The fourth decision box requires an action (Figure 2).

Be Positive and Stay (PS)	Be Positive and Leave (PL)
Be Negative and Leave (NL)	But She *Can't* Be Negative and Stay (NS)

Figure 2

Depending on the situation and the person I am working with, I sometimes use "Happy" and "Sad" in place of "Positive" and

"Negative." When a manager or other employee accepts that he or she is in the "Negative and Stay" box, I then explain that one of two things needs to change: attitude, or place of employment. As the result of the decision grid discussion, some do change their attitudes; others choose to leave; and a few over the years have chosen to simply remain negative, which left me no choice but to assist them on to new positions at other companies.

If a manager *can't* do a job due to lack of knowledge or proper training for skill development, the situation can be helped. If a manager *won't* do a job due to negative attitude, it's time for him or her to move on.

Check the Guidebook

Negative thinking produces negative assumptions, actions, and results. I worked in a company that lost two years of progress because the president thought that he would not be successful in asking the corporation for control of a key program that was eroding company sales. When he finally did ask two years later, the corporation gave him control of the program with little resistance. Sadly, two years of forward motion had been lost because one leader allowed negative thinking to produce continued negative action.

There's a great example of the effect of negative thinking in the Guidebook where the boss (Moses) commissioned a group of leaders to assess the environmental conditions that would be found once an unfriendly takeover was complete. The leaders reported excellent conditions, but because of their negative thinking, they convinced each other that a takeover attempt would fail. They infected the entire organization with negativism, which produced a team of people who grumbled against the takeover.

The boss at corporate headquarters (God) heard the grumbling and held the people accountable for their negative behavior. The takeover didn't happen until a full generation later, when under a new leader (Joshua) it was discovered that the inhabitants of the area subject to the original takeover had been terrified of being taken over and were ready to concede. It would have been an easy acquisition. The negative thinkers and their negative assumptions led to action paralysis, adding 40 years to the time before the original goal would be reached.

The Guidebook also illustrates that negative thinking is contagious. When God gave the Children of Israel their laws of military service, he gave them instruction that prior to going into battle, the leaders should ask if anyone was afraid. Those who were afraid were to be released to go home so that the rest of the troops wouldn't be contaminated by their negativism.

On the positive side, the Guidebook gives advice on how to avoid negative thoughts. It directs us to think about things that are right, pure, lovely, admirable, excellent and praiseworthy. When admirable and excellent thoughts fill the mind, admirable and excellent actions will be the output.

Fold 'Em or Hold 'Em?

If a manager thinks that a project will fail, it will. The head of a department at a company where I formerly worked made a detailed presentation to the executive staff on an aggressive plan that required resources and financial commitment. At the end of the presentation, the president of the company asked, "On a scale of one to ten, what do you think are the chances of this plan succeeding?" The manager replied, "Oh, I'd say about a six." Everyone in the room could have easily heard a pin drop. The department head had pitched a program that he didn't believe in; it turned out to be a career-ending moment for the manager.

When a manager believes wholeheartedly in a project plan, it will be easy to promote in a positive and enthusiastic manner. But even the best presentation effort may not receive immediate peer and executive buy in. If a manager remains passionate about a plan but is having difficulty in getting the commitment needed, there is a three-word phrase I learned from a highly successful sales professional that will be an encouragement:

Persistence Overcomes Resistance

Women have a gift of being persistent. One of the stories in the Guidebook is that of Delilah, who got what she wanted by pestering

Samson daily with her words. One of Jesus' parables told of the persistent widow who pleaded over and over again until the judge granted her the justice she so persistently sought. The judge made his ruling in her favor so that she wouldn't eventually wear him out. One company president told me that one of the things he admired most about me was my tenacity. The head of a company would prefer a persistent manager any day of the week over one who gives up easily.

Making Lemonade out of a Lemon

At one point in my career, I was offered a position that was a non-limelight job that had real potential to take me down a different career path. Even though it was a promotion, I would have hated the assignment. I would have felt hemmed in and stuck behind a desk. While it was a sweet opportunity for the right person, I viewed the position as a sour lemon for me.

At the same point in time, another female manager, who thrived on behind-the-scenes projects, told me that she was being offered a role that would require her to travel and give public presentations. She had no desire to move her career in that direction and also felt like she was handed a lemon.

We worked together to squeeze both lemons into lemonade. We met with the key decision maker on the positions and proposed an opportunity swap. We had worked out the advantages to the company and the specific advantages to the decision-maker. As a result, he reversed the job offers. Both female managers joyfully continued on their planned career paths. No whining; just shining.

Difficult People

Sooner or later in your career you will interact with a colleague who seems unbearable. It could be a style issue that clashes with yours, or it could be that the colleague simply doesn't care how obnoxious his or her behavior may be. Some choose to avoid such a person as often as they can, but selecting this tactic often means hurting your own career advancement. Some choose to use strategic whining, soliciting as much negative support from others as possible, which only causes them to feel even more bitter toward the person. Strategic whining is a career-hindering move.

I took a course once that changed my whole approach toward difficult people. The course required me to select a person with whom I was having a particularly difficult time and to list three ways in which we were different. I really enjoyed that assignment; I had a hard time stopping at just three differences. Then, I was asked to list three things that I admired about that person, a much more difficult task. I realized that I did admire this person's achievements and business savvy, and came up with three specifics. Finally, to my horror, I was asked to list three ways that the two of us were *alike*. It was very difficult to admit—let alone write down—that there were at least three ways that we were indeed very similar.

As a result of the exercise, I developed a greater sensitivity to what might be making this person tick. I have to admit that I began to view him differently once I became aware that our conflict could have been caused by our sameness and not by our opposite qualities.

There was still one more assignment to go. I was asked to begin to pray for this person. I honestly didn't think I could. But, what I found was that when I prayed for him, although he didn't change, my attitude did. That's when I came to understand that I was responsible for how I reacted to him. My focus changed from complaining to managing our interaction together. Our working relationship improved, and although we no longer work together, we greet each other with a hug and swap business stories over lunch when we periodically get together.

The 24-Hour Rule

The whining-prevention technique for which I have been thanked most often is one I call the "24-Hour Rule." I have used it often in business and have taught it to others. It has saved many a manager, particularly those who use instant messaging on the computer, from slipping off the ladder and sliding down one of those slippery chutes. Picture how a manager might react to the following scenarios:

- An email arrives, copied to the manager's boss, with flawed information that positions the manager in a very poor light.

- A manager is assigned to a time-consuming team project without her input or permission.
- Someone tells a woman manager that another person has suggested to several people that she (the woman manager) is to blame for a failed project.

Circumstances like these strike emotional nerves. There are two typical reactions. Some immediately begin a public cranking and whining campaign about the idiot who authored the email, the project assignment, or rumor. The other reaction, rage, often leads to physically stomping down the hall to confront the offender with a poorly thought-out attack that bites back, or a hastily written email response that adds more fuel to the already raging fire.

The whole key to the 24-hour rule is to stay in control and to take a specific period of time to plan the most effective way to confront or respond—without emotion guiding your thoughts. When emotion is the guiding force a woman tends to back others into a corner from which they might come out swinging more verbal or written punches. When a manager lets 24 hours pass before reacting, she will have time to review her gut reaction in a new light. The action that she takes once the response is carefully thought through will differ greatly from the initial emotional reaction.

Sometimes a manager doesn't have 24 hours before she has to respond. She may have only 24 minutes; maybe even just 24 seconds. She needs to take whatever time she has available to push out that initial negative gut reaction and replace it with positive thinking.

It All Comes Down to Self-Control

To really shine as a professional, a woman needs to manage her gift of emotional response through self-control. The life and work benefits of self-control are many: less personal stress, effectively planned reactions and responses, a reputation of excellence, persistent and consistent forward motion toward goal achievement, and improved career opportunity.

A manager might not be able to control the business circumstances, but she can control her reaction to them.

A woman controls the decision as to how she will respond to negative input, circumstances, and events. Whining leads to a career chute; shining, using strategy and self-control, points toward the next ladder.

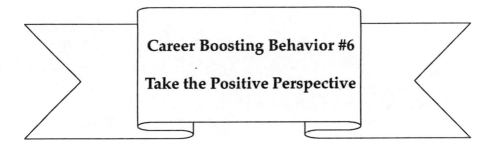

Career Boosting Behavior #6

Take the Positive Perspective

SABOTAGE #7

Key Concepts

- A balanced life increases career success
- A career is not a competition
- All aspects of a woman's personal and business life need to be based on the same core values

SABOTAGE #7

Living An Unbalanced Life

All Work and No Interests

I was single when I began climbing the middle of the management ladder. I had somehow determined that I needed to put every bit of life energy into my job if I were going to someday achieve my goal of becoming an upper-management executive. I was at my desk working before any other manager each day. I worked a twelve-hour day, frequently took work home, and was in on Saturdays for at least half a day. I had few, if any, outside interests.

Because I was consumed by work, I didn't realize that I had buried myself in tasks that no longer contributed to the accomplishment of my goals and objectives against which I'd be measured at review time. Even though I was doing many things right, they weren't the right things. My self-imposed heavy workload was crushing my creative energies. While I wanted a reputation as an up-and-coming dynamic contributor to company growth, the reputation I was cultivating was one of being someone who works really hard. I was sabotaging my ability to advance by allowing work to exhaust my energy.

When a woman leader's life becomes consumed by work,
she loses sight of the next rung of her career ladder.

All Interests, No Priorities

I studied successful upper-level managers and discovered that there were several things that they had in common. Most of them were married with children. Most had lots of outside activities including volunteer work in the community. Many networked with other managers both in and outside the industry. Every one of them had a full life outside the office.

Since I wanted to become an upper-level manager, I set my sights on achieving a better life balance. First, I eliminated nonessential work tasks. As I took less work home and reduced the extra time spent at the office by a couple of hours a day, I made room for outside interests. I even managed to squeeze in a husband and a son.

With so much more packed into my life, I began to struggle with priorities. Career seemed to have a continuous hold on the number one position, with the rest of my life activities jammed in behind in random order. To sort out a priority system, I needed to determine what should be my number one concern. I consulted the Guidebook and saw that even before Eve was in the picture, Adam was given work responsibilities, so work must be important. But we also get a picture of a natural order for life's priorities. I discovered that the way to straighten out my own priorities was to make a conscious effort to place God at the top and then follow his defined order.

Who's the Boss?

As I was told that I was being downsized from a company, one of the persons charged with counseling me asked if I was doing all right after receiving the news. I responded with these words: "Friend, my "boss" never sat in the large office on mahogany row. My boss is up there (pointing up), and it's moments like this when you live your faith." I am so grateful that those were the words that came out in response to the question. God was not always in first place in my life, but I'm sure glad he had top billing on that day.

I know of career women who believe that a woman's faith should be checked at the main door before she enters her place of employment to begin her workday, and she should reclaim her faith only after quitting time. Their belief is flawed. "Thou Shalt Not Steal" means both paying for all items you pick up in a department store as well as putting down only legitimate business expense charges on a company expense report. Life at work and a life of faith both need to be based on the same values. If they are not, the woman will be forced to live a schizophrenic life with one set of values reserved for work and one set of ethical behaviors reserved for use in her personal life outside the office.

A woman's values are an important part of her actions. A woman in a leadership position will suffer from self-imposed stress when her work actions do not match her ethical beliefs.

Spouse and Career

Having an awesome husband has proven to be a career advantage. Whenever I describe my husband, I tell people that he holds my kite string. I'm up there in all my color sailing around the sky, capturing the wind, and seizing the moment. My husband holds onto the thin cord that keeps me from flying off and crashing to the ground. He works with me, letting the string in and out as needed so that I can enjoy my experience to the fullest.

A woman who is not married can be at a career disadvantage. Without a partner working with her to maintain balance among her life activities, work can consume her. If she's not careful, she'll end up taking a slow ride down a long chute by putting in long hours, taking work home at night, and clouding her career vision.

When I became a field sales manager, I spent a minimum of four days a week out of town and on the road. I was determined to achieve the sales director of the year award, and since I had the most number of field reps and the highest quota assignment, I felt that I needed to put in extra effort to achieve my goal. Weekends soon became a regular part of my work schedule. When I was home, I would fall asleep on the sofa shortly after dinner.

My wonderfully supportive husband asked me to sit down with him one day and said the following: "I can see that this new position is taking its toll on you. Think about it: on a normal week, you leave the house Monday morning and when you I see you again, you enter the house exhausted. Do you realize that you have been away from home three out of the last four weekends? This position is not only taking a toll on you, it's taking a toll on our family."

My husband was absolutely right. I was out of balance again. While it was hard to hear his words, and even harder to admit that I had gotten out of control, I agreed to readjust how I was pursuing that sales director award goal by working smarter rather than harder. One of the changes that I made was to develop peer leaders within the sales group who began supervising the smaller weekend projects. As a result, my out-of-town weekend commitments were cut in half. Thanks to my husband giving that kite string a hard tug, I avoided impending burnout and still achieved sales director of the year.

Married women in management who don't utilize their husbands as a strategic work advantage are limiting their careers. Communication with her spouse is key. He needs to know that she values his input on business issues. He also needs to know that while God may have a firm hold on first place, he has a lock on the silver medal position. It's a great benefit that a woman in management can have access—in person or by phone—to a personal consultant on both business and life issues. Her spouse's inside scoop on what a male colleague's perspective might be on an issue is invaluable when dealing with men customers.

Adding Children to the Equation

I have found that most career women with young children at home manage their situations very well. As a middle-level manager I needed to fill an entry-level supervisor position. I interviewed a young woman within the company who, at the time of the interview, was just short of seven months pregnant. If I hired her, I would have my hands full in covering for her during her maternity leave. I would also be taking a risk that she might not return to work. Since her character was part of what caused me to interview her in the first place, I chose to believe her when she said that she had no thoughts of being a stay-at-home mom. I took the risk and hired her.

She returned to work as promised. It was never easy for her to balance two children, a husband and a demanding work position, but she did. She stayed late when the job required it, even if it meant creative management of childcare. Her work performance was second to none. Years later after we had both moved on to other positions, she applied for an open management position which reported to me. I didn't hesitate to hire her.

Have It All; Don't Do It All

The key for a woman to continue a successful career while managing small children at home is to get help. The superwoman/supermom characterization is a myth. A career woman will be unable to strike an effective balance if she tries to manage it all as a lone ranger.

I have known many women leaders who have successfully returned to their careers shortly after having a child. During my sales management days, I had two highly successful career women on my team. Both of them had several children. In order to maintain a balance between work and home, they both contracted for the services of live-in nannies. Each woman outsourced, or more accurately insourced, the care of the children during the workday as well as for the evenings and weekends when her job required her to travel.

Many of the women who have worked with and for me had the support of family who provided child care during the workday. In the absence of local family, some women placed their children with trustworthy stay-at-home-mom friends during working hours. Others chose to place their preschool children in day care. While the method of child care varied for each of these women, they all had implemented some sort of support system that enabled them to balance work and home.

Good companies assist career women with creative solutions to child care needs. Some offer on-site child care. Some companies allow women managers to work out of their homes one or two days a week. How a company supports women with children can be an influencing factor when women of childbearing age are evaluating the pros and cons of staying with their current employer versus seeking a new employment possibility.

Children as a Disability?

A woman has one rather obvious piece of uniqueness when it comes to having children. She is the only gender built to bear them. In addition to being uniquely designed to bear children, women have also been uniquely created and equipped for nurturing children during their childhood. Nurturing a child is a wonderful and high calling. A woman gets but one opportunity to instill foundational values in her preschool children. More career women might make a decision to stay home with their children during their preschool years if they understood the following fact:

Taking a break from your career doesn't mean that you quit the game.

Choosing to step off the career ladder for a time to raise children is a gutsy move, but one to be admired and respected. It all comes down to how highly a woman values her personal interaction in the day-to-day instruction and guidance given to her preschool children.

What About the Money?

I have heard a number of career women say that they would like to stay home with their children but they can't afford it. In particular, single moms have a double dilemma. As the only wage earner, a single mom must work outside the home, and since she works outside the home, paid child care often consumes a major portion of her paycheck. While two-income families may feel that it is necessary to maintain both incomes to meet their current expenses, they do have the option of a making a good lifestyle for themselves on a single income. By choosing to live on one income, they can reduce many of the expenses associated with both of them going to work each day and also eliminate paid child care.

My husband worked for a company that was experiencing declining revenues for several years. When the company offered a voluntary layoff package, he declined. However, we decided to prepare for the next opportunity. We started to bank his entire salary and covered our expenses from my salary alone for one year. When the next offering was made, my husband had his request in immediately. When he stopped working, we found that our everyday expenses dropped significantly. Auto expense, lunches out during the workday, and dry cleaning are three areas where we experienced considerable and immediate savings. The net effect was that we felt little impact on our lifestyle. A married woman in management who decides to take a child care break from her career may be surprised at how doable living on one income can be.

It's a Career, Not a Competition

My husband and I enjoy driving around the beautiful wine country north of San Francisco. We plan where we want to end up, and we let the path to get there unfold as we go. We stop at attractions as they present themselves and don't lock ourselves into a time schedule.

However, whenever we take a long driving trip using major highways, it's very difficult for me to stop for more than a quick break at a rest stop. I somehow place myself in a contest with other drivers. Once we have passed them, I get disturbed at the thought that if we stop for a break those same cars might move ahead of us. It's ridiculous for me to feel that way. I am not competing against other drivers; I am traveling to a destination goal, and the pace of others really has nothing to do with my trip.

The way that I feel toward other highway drivers is exactly how some career women feel when they contemplate having children. They fear that if they stop to raise a family, someone else will charge ahead of them in some sort of a career competition. It is true that if a women returns to the same work position after taking a leave of absence to raise her children to school age, she will find that others may have advanced, though her career reentry compensation level has not. A woman measuring her career progress against others who happen to be moving on the same career path makes about as much sense as me measuring my trip progress against other drivers. In each situation, only individual progress and attainment of personal goals really matters.

A financial manager friend stepped away from a thriving career to be a stay-at-home mom with her third and final child. She expressed to me that it was not easy to do, but she took a step of faith that God would provide for her career. Sure enough, when her child reached school age, she landed an incredible management opportunity. God did his part, but she also did hers by staying current with industry trends and by keeping her skills up-to-date, readying her for reentry.

The Opportunities Are Endless

Women who struggle with the thought of taking a child-rearing break need to consider that the position a woman leaves is not her only option when she chooses to return to work. There are amazing opportunities open to career women who are willing to invest some of the time they spend at home into new areas while on their career break.

A female manager I worked with was known for her exceptional work expertise; in fact, her company had come to depend heavily on her special skills. After years devoted to moving up the career ladder, she and her husband decided to adopt a child. She partnered her decision to adopt with the decision to be a stay-at-home mom.

She negotiated with her place of employment to become an independent contractor and to provide service out of her home. She worked online with the baby at her side and created her own flex hours around the baby's needs. She loved the freedom of working from home and continued to make a terrific income.

Businesswomen who take a break to raise their children are forming investment clubs and spend a portion of their day managing their financial portfolios. Some women leaders choose to enhance their education online as they stay home with their preschoolers. There are even organizations for career women who are taking a child-rearing sabbatical. Taking a career break on behalf of her children can be a woman's time of real personal growth.

Older and Still Challenging

Career women with older children continue to have balance challenges. A last-minute emergency business trip replaces a mother's promise to her daughter of attending her play. A customer meeting runs three hours late and she misses her son's first touchdown.

When our son was a young teenager, I was on a business trip in Asia. Rumors abounded that terrorists would be looking for Americans traveling by plane. I cancelled my scheduled stop to India when the U.S. issued a traveler's warning midtrip. When I called home that evening, I heard the stress in my son's voice as he expressed his fears for my safety. My heart was heavy the rest of the trip knowing I was causing my son to be so anxious.

At the close of each school year the stress level can soar when, added to the normal latchkey child concerns, a woman is called on to manage her children as they participate in summer sports and special programs offered for them. Managing a successful career while managing a successful household is not for the faint of heart.

Others in Life

Others that need attention in a career woman's life include parents, siblings, extended family, friends, and community. All of these people can provide enriching relationships that can round out a businesswoman's life. The "other" category is usually an especially high priority category for single women in management who do not have the responsibilities associated with having a spouse or children. A few good friends with whom to share life's experiences are much needed to prevent a career from becoming an all-consuming life force, which yields burnout and limited life experiences.

A woman's participation in carefully selected organizations can produce career benefits as well as life enrichment. Continuous exposure to a single workplace environment can produce incestuous thought. Management methods used are often particular to a company's culture. Being involved in outside organizations gives a new perspective for management theory and problem solving that can be directly integrated into a woman's work life.

Career women should choose outside associations that in some way contribute to her career goals. Each of the three organizations in which I currently participate has increased my work effectiveness through the development of my knowledge base, skill set, and people network. My longest running association is as a volunteer crisis counselor. The counseling skills that I learned through this volunteer organization have a positive and powerful impact on how I handle work relationships in general, and also how I manage employees who are in difficult situations. Time commitment to this organization is one evening per week plus three or four two-hour training meetings annually.

After developing an understanding of the impact that counseling provides, I joined the board of directors of another non-profit counseling center that serves the community at large. After a few years, I became a board officer. I continue to gain new insight into improved methods of running a business as each board member contributes his or her experiences. Time commitment is a two-hour board meeting six times per year, with two to three special meetings annually.

The third association is one that I founded. The organization is for women in management and gives them the opportunity to network with other career women who share their values while providing access to low cost seminars and presentations by area business leaders. Meetings are held quarterly with a seminar or special event annually. As a result of my commitment to this organization I have developed many new contacts and connections.

Each organization in which a career woman participates needs to be one which supports her career objectives. In addition to deciding which associations to pursue she must determine what role within them is best for her. The rungs of the career ladder become easier to reach when a woman supports her career through associations that build skills and connections.

Women and Faith

The woman with personal faith positioned in first place will frame her conduct and behavior on high ground. She will have a firm foundation on which to base her personal and work ethics. A growing number of companies are recognizing the benefits of having a leadership team that follows ethical business practices. These companies are establishing policies to try to instill ethical behavior in their employees. A woman who bases her behavior on the Guidebook doesn't need a company policy to regulate her morals and her ethics.

The Guidebook portrays the importance of having a prioritized connection between personal faith and work in this way: "As long as he sought the Lord, God gave him success." Over the years I have come to realize that God is the best business partner you can have.

Women and Spouses

Some of the work benefits of having access to a husband's point of view have been mentioned, but far more important is having a husband as career partner. My husband and I spend our first minutes of each day sharing a cup of coffee while we watch the morning news, weather, and commute conditions. We discuss our plans and schedules for the day.

We are each other's support system. He supports my individual goals and I support his. We team together on common goals. We often bounce business scenarios off each other to confirm a conclusion or to get a different perspective. Not long ago we encouraged each other to get started on an exercise program and to change our eating habits. As a result, we lost several bowling balls worth of weight, which gave me more public appearance confidence and gave him lower blood pressure. Each of us committed to support the other and both benefited.

Women and Children

Children can not only bring great joy to a career woman's life, but they can also add to her career skills. My son taught me so much that made me a better manager. He taught me how to answer questions logically not emotionally, because that was how he received and processed information. He taught me not to exaggerate, because he always needed supporting facts to be provided. And now that he is a man, I am awed by the wisdom that he interjects into our family and business discussions.

I once heard that a good test to see if a career woman is achieving balance is for her to listen how her children describe her to their friends. If her children depict her as tired, cranky, and never home, she may need to reevaluate her priorities. In presenting the picture of a balanced career woman, the Guidebook states that "her children arise and call her blessed". I was personally blessed when I opened my most recent Mother's Day card to find that my son had written, "Thank you for always working to make me successful." A career woman who is achieving balance will see the evidence in her children.

Women and Others

The mystery of a woman's investment in others is that she gets back far more than she gives. When she plays a significant role in an organization because of her value that she brings to the table, she broadens her reputation and increases her networking opportunities.

When she helps a friend to overcome a difficult life issue, she learns new people skills that can be applied on the job.

The amount of time invested in the "other" area of a woman's life needs to be carefully managed. Others can put significant demands on a career woman's time. Learning to say "no" to avoid overload is a great gift that a woman can give to herself. I was once counseled that I needed to stop stepping up to every open volunteer leadership role that presented itself. By saying "yes" to every opportunity, I was headed for leadership overload while denying others opportunities to develop as leaders.

In Search of Balance

The Guidebook recommends that we manage our energy that we spend in trying to race up the career ladder:

> *Do not wear yourself out to get rich; have the wisdom to show restraint.*
> —*Proverbs 23:4*

To achieve personal balance, all aspects of a woman's life should be based on the same core values. A woman will enhance her career opportunities when she balances her priorities. To achieve maximum reach for a secure grasp on the next rung of the ladder, a woman should consider her career in this way:

> *Faith directing it, spouse enhancing it, children intensifying it,*
> *and others enriching it.*

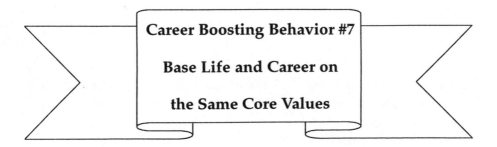

Career Boosting Behavior #7

Base Life and Career on

the Same Core Values

SABOTAGE #8

Key Concepts

- Planning improves risk success rates
- Risk needs to be managed
- Change is inevitable, growth within change is optional

SABOTAGE #8

Running from Risk

The Comfort Zone

There is a certain reckless abandon with which women new to management approach opportunities. They are usually overconfident about their skills and abilities. As soon as they move up one rung on their career ladder they immediate begin reaching for the next rung.

As time passes and as life situations inevitably change, most women managers become more cautious about career decisions. A woman who actively manages her career carefully and deliberately will enjoy career progress. However, overly cautious behavior can easily lead to the creation of a risk-averse mindset, which creates a career comfort zone that she strives to protect. A woman whose cautious behavior fortifies her comfort zone no longer embraces the risk that is an integral part of upward career movement. Rather than enthusiastically welcoming risk, she fearfully runs from it.

If a woman's niche has become a place to hide, the time has come for her to reevaluate her career objectives. When she finds that protecting her comfort zone has become more satisfying than stretching for new challenges, her career path has come to an official dead end. While taking risks is invigorating, hiding in the comfort zone is enervating, extinguishing her desire to generate career moves.

> *"A ship in a safe harbor is safe, but that is not what a ship is built for."*
> —William Shedd

When Risk Chooses You

As a young office supervisor, I was recruited for a position as a buyer in the New York fashion industry. It was an exciting opportunity to learn the business from the bottom up that required me to relocate to the Big Apple. After weighing the pros and cons of the opportunity, I realized I hadn't prepared financially for this type of risk. I had little savings built up and was cash strapped. The opportunity cost to get in the game was beyond my means and I declined the position.

Years later, I was offered a field sales position, a career opportunity that I had never even imagined might be a career possibility. I had no previous sales experience other than a summer job at a local department store. It would mean leaving the safety of my office surroundings to step into a new world of an unstructured work environment requiring tremendous self-discipline. I greatly respected the sales manager who made the offer and was confident that he would commit his resources to help me.

But, once again I hadn't prepared for an opportunity that brought with it a fair amount of risk, so I turned it down. My desired career path had become a comfort zone. The thought of deviating from my determined career goals just didn't compute. My career vision was nearsighted and self-limiting instead of farsighted and flexible.

This was a huge opportunity lost. Had I thought it through more carefully, I might have understood the impact that having field sales experience would have had on my ability to achieve my long-range career goals. As a result of not adding direct sales territory management to my portfolio, I added rungs to my success ladder which made it harder to climb. I had missed gaining broader experience that could have enabled me to achieve a senior management position much sooner than I did.

Planning Reduces the Risk

A number of years ago I was contacted by an international organization to present a speech to a number of industry leaders. I was intimidated by the thought that I was being sought out as an expert. I felt a sense of panic. I would need to step way outside my comfort zone to do this presentation, and I doubted my ability to do an effective job. I bounced the idea off my mentor, who not only encouraged me by pointing out the benefit to my career, but insisted that I do it.

As I planned out the speech, I felt my panic level decrease. I rehearsed. I tweaked the presentation. I rehearsed again until I knew it cold. By the time I was walking up to the podium to deliver the speech, my anxiety had turned into that invigorating feeling that you get just before you do a great presentation. Through effective planning, I managed risk down to size.

Embracing Risk

One of the companies I worked for merged with another company headquartered in a different city and state. My work world was about to be turned upside down. I was asked to work on the transition team, as was my direct counterpart from the other company. As I sat across the table from him in his office during our initial meeting I said, "Look, I don't know if either one of us will have a job after this transition is complete, but I only know how to give 100% to anything I'm asked to do. You have my commitment that I will be working to ensure the new company's success." He extended his right hand and responded, "I'm right there with you."

As we worked on forming the newly combined company, I began to get a feel for what options might be open to me. I identified four possible outcomes:

1. I could be asked to relocate to the new location in my present or a similar position.
2. I could be offered a position in another area of the company that would allow me to work locally.
3. I could be asked to leave as redundant positions were downsized.
4. I could find a job now with another organization.

While I had initially thought that being asked to leave would be the worst of the four possibilities, it emerged as my number two most desired outcome. The least attractive option was the relocation, since my husband's career was at a point where he needed to stay local and I also didn't relish moving further from our son's college. I wanted the experience of completing a merger transition, so I rejected seeking a position with another company. A new position with the same company that would keep me local would be best for my current life circumstances.

By thinking through the potential outcomes, I felt no fear of change and minimized the risk factors. I planned for all four outcomes. As I worked to form the new company, I was unencumbered by fear of risk so I could keep an eye peeled for opportunity. The opportunity materialized that would give me new experience, would facilitate the development of new skills, and would allow me to stay local. I targeted that position in my sights and when the dust settled, I was offered what I viewed as the perfect outcome: a regional sales management position that included my home geographic area.

Choosing Risk

Risk surrounds a career woman. In any outside job search there is risk that the new company she decides to join might turn out to be a lot like the old company she was so eager to leave. A woman can reduce the risk by investigating the new company's philosophy including its commitment to the customer, its company culture, and its track record of women who had successful careers with the company.

When a woman targets a new position, she should become involved in more than just the pursuit of the challenge; she should be committed to it and should demonstrate it by taking on risk. She might send a short letter to the CEO of a company where she wants to move her career ladder, listing the top five or six things she'll bring to the company that will impact the bottom line. I know I'd have a closer look at somebody with the spunk to send such a letter to me.

Risky situations don't always come in the form of a potential new position. A woman may see or be the recipient of an injustice that needs correction. Despite rules against it, taking a stand brings the risk of retaliation by management. A woman manager who understands that there will be risk in taking action and still chooses to do it needs to consider how strongly she believes in her cause and how much she is willing to risk. My son once taught me a great truth that gave me confidence in pursuing a just solution for a work issue:

Beware of the person who has nothing to lose.

At one point in my career, I thought through the potential outcomes of pursuing an equal pay for equal work issue. I first examined myself to make sure that it was not just my pride that was causing me to take my stand on the issue. Satisfied that it was not, I made certain that I had accurate facts, not rumors, and documented a time line of events.

I then thought through possible outcomes. I felt certain that I'd be accused of playing the discrimination card, which might lead to unfavorable career consequences. The fact is:

You can't play a card that somebody hasn't already put in the deck.

If a woman is dealt a discrimination card, she needs to determine if and how she's going to play it. In my situation, I realized that a possible outcome would be for the company to ask me to leave. I decided that if that were to happen, it would be worth the risk if the injustice could be corrected for other women who would follow. I was financially prepared for a job loss outcome. With nothing to lose and justice to gain, I went for it.

I was not prepared for the great lengths to which two decision makers on the issue went to try to first discourage and then discredit me. They tried diversionary tactics with unsupported attacks on my job performance. Persistence required more patience and more stamina than I ever thought I had. But I hung tight and stayed with it until the company changed its position. Persistence overcomes resistance.

Choosing the Length of the Ladder

Women have the freedom to decide that they don't want to pay the price of admission required for upper management. The higher a woman manager goes up the ladder, the higher the risk becomes. Stepping into upper management means that in some industries a woman can expect to change positions every two to three years. The higher she goes on the upper-management career ladder, the harder it will be to find jobs within her same geographic area. She will ever be in search of balance between her home life and her work life as she travels more, is relocated more, has more business dinners, and meets with more clients after normal business hours on time that used to belong to the family.

A woman who desires a career in middle management is to be encouraged. Most of the women customer service and support managers that I have known love their jobs. They have a feeling of great satisfaction knowing that they are serving customers and enjoy working with the employee teams that they lead. Good middle managers have an advantage over senior managers in that they can usually find new positions locally. I have known many women who have spent their careers in middle management and who find their lives balanced and greatly satisfying. They are women who understand what career success really means.

The Middle-Management Career Trap

Some women managers never grasp that their value to the company goes up with their ability to develop others through coaching and mentoring. I know of manager who worked almost every Saturday morning when the office was closed. She tried to protect her staff from pressure by taking it all on herself. However, as she protected them, she not only prevented them from developing new strengths, she trapped herself in a web of tactical tasks. Who is making her department's strategic growth plans if everybody is doing the task work?

Middle-level women managers need to guard carefully against trapping themselves in a comfortable role. Skills and abilities need to be in a constant growth pattern. Change will be viewed as less of a risk when a woman prepares for it by developing new ways to contribute to the organization. Resistance to change is a common but career-strangling response. We self-impose constraints by trying to maintain the status quo; the problem is that there is no such thing as status quo in business.

Change is inevitable; a career woman's growth within that change is optional.

One of my most mind-boggling relationships was one I had with a bright, educated single female manager who absolutely refused to grow. She was a dedicated employee who had stepped up to a supervisor position from an administrative role. I saw great potential in her and attempted to establish a mentoring relationship with her. But I found that she was quite comfortable doing things the way she had always done them. She was focused on how much work she did rather than what she and her team contributed to the bottom line of the company.

I tried all my best techniques in giving what I thought were well-supported arguments for a change in her behavior that would position her for growth within the company. I gave her suggestions for how to justify the head count in her department, warning her that she was endangering her team by not being able to financially justify their existence. The net result was that she continued to protect her comfort zone at all costs.

Over time, organizational changes resulted in a new reporting relationship for this manager. The new department head took her resistance to change as management weakness and her inability to justify head count cost her most of her staff. The title of supervisor was revoked and to keep a position with the company, she was forced to absorb the work previously done by the staff who was eliminated. Comfort zones can cause a painful slide down a long chute.

Checking the Guidebook

Just about everybody knows the Guidebook story of Moses leading the Israelites to the Promised Land. I found it interesting to note that Moses doesn't exactly jump at the risk involved with putting it all on the line and heading for an unknown land based on a promise. Even though it is God who makes the promise, Moses tries everything to get out of answering his call to leadership. He uses the "why me?" approach, the "what if they don't believe me or listen to me?" approach, and finally the "I'm not a good speaker" approach. His boss (God) gives Moses the resources he needs to minimize the risk. Once Moses sees that by using those resources he can manage the risk, he becomes a great leader.

Each step up a new rung on a career ladder comes with a degree of risk. Most leaders accept the fact that there is risk in making a career move. Effective leaders don't just accept risk; they manage it.

Survival as a Tactic

From time to time a woman's career strategy may shift into survival mode, which can be fine if it is a temporary tactic. Survival mode kicks in when the head of your department leaves and the company begins a search for external rather than internal talent to fill the position. Survival mode can be triggered when the company has just downsized and a new president is coming on board. A woman focuses on survival when she has a significant work anniversary date coming within a year that brings added stock option benefits just as the company decides to change direction.

Even during survival mode there is risk that needs to be managed. The key to managing risk when the temporary goal is to survive is the same key used to manage a controlling-style boss:

Results, Not Efforts

Only demonstrated results—not great and marvelous efforts—will enable you to stick around while reorganization possibilities are being sorted out.

Survival mode needs to be employed only as a tactic that is part of an overall career strategy. A career woman needs to be weighing her options and taking appropriate action to prepare for her next career move. If a woman chooses survival as her long-term business goal rather than as a short-term tactic, it will become a career-finishing strategy.

Times Have Changed

Years ago, a layoff could be devastating to a career. No one who was thought to be of any value in an organization was ever laid off. Landing a position with another company was difficult if not impossible after a layoff especially for those in management careers. As a result, managers often took a ride down a long chute as they made poor reemployment decisions that took them further from their career goals.

Every woman needs to realize there is a high probability that she will be downsized at least once during her career. Potential employers no longer view someone who has been laid off as someone who has no value. Having managed several layoffs, I can tell you that while layoffs can sometimes be used to weed out underproductive or problem employees, most layoffs are due to business downturns or new strategic direction. Well-managed layoffs eliminate positions that unfortunately often have good women assigned to them. Accepting that there is always the risk of a layoff is important; preparing for it and managing it is essential.

Planning for Risk

Successful career women plan for the inevitable risks that will come. They prepare for better positions within their organization. They design a road map to find a similar or higher position with another company in case their present company opportunities dry up or the present company changes direction. They even formulate plans to make a life change that will enable them to do something completely different should business conditions warrant a career change.

A woman can prepare for taking risks in seeking better job assignments within her company and within new companies by asking herself what skills and education she lacks that might prevent her from securing a higher position. For example, higher-level positions require giving presentations to senior management. A woman desiring to move to the next level would be advised to hone her public speaking skills through seminars, classes, or organizations.

Education has become increasingly more important when searching for a new position, even within a woman's current company. Of the fifty best women in business for the state in which I live, forty-two of the women business leaders had a four-year college degree. Of the eight who did not, half had an associate's degree or some college.

To advance within her own organization and to prepare for a potential future with another company, a woman should ask herself if her skills are up to date and marketable. Despite having a bachelor's and even a master's degree, her skills will become quickly outdated if she is not attending seminars and courses which use case studies as well as those which prepare her to take advantage of new technology.

A career woman sabotages her ability to seek risk if she is not involved in a networking organization. It is both *what* a woman knows and *who* she knows that will create situations which she can choose to pursue.

Be Ready

My favorite mentor gave me a simple two-word piece of advice that has encouraged me and enabled me to address risk:

Be Ready

He first stated those succinct words to me in response to my expression of distress when, just a few days after he hired me, he made an "oh, by the way" comment that he needed me to prepare a full training program on all products within thirty days. On top of that, he was sending me on the road to five countries to present it and I was to leave on day thirty-one.

My entire credibility with international distributors would be on the line. I remember thinking that since he was willing to take the risk on me, I'd better plan to "be ready." I was ready in time, and the training trip was highly successful. I have remembered those two simple words before each executive and key client presentation that I have ever made. Risk is minimized when a career woman is prepared.

Risk Management

As with all areas of a woman's life, risk can be managed, too. She manages it by accepting it as part of her climb on her career ladder, minimizing it through preparation and planning, and seeking it in her pursuit of career excellence.

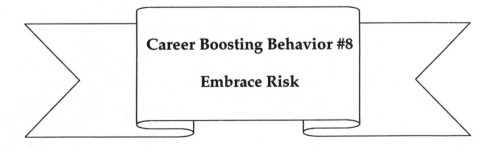

Career Boosting Behavior #8

Embrace Risk

SABOTAGE #9

Key Concepts

- A career needs to be actively managed
- There are always signs when it is time to make a career move
- People will always remember how you conduct yourself when leaving a company

SABOTAGE #9

Staying Too Long

Knowing When to Go

"Why do I always stay too long? I did it at my last company, and I'm doing it now."

The talented sales manager who made this comment to me struggles with the timing of career moves. I remember thinking I would know that it was time to make a change when I felt that I had nothing more to give to a company or to a certain position. I never got that feeling. No matter what position I held, I never felt that I had contributed all that I had to offer. I came to realize that a woman who determines that her next career move will be based on a certain "feeling" will stay in her current position long past its value to her career.

Women stay in a position or with a company too long when they are not proactively managing their careers based on a vision of where they want their careers to go. A woman will find herself stuck on the same rung of her career ladder, which may be rotting out from under her, if she is not continuously evaluating career growth opportunities within as well as outside her current place of employment.

If a woman thinks she might have stayed too long, she is probably right. If so, she has stopped climbing the ladder and is simply clinging to it.

Where's the Party?

There was a time when a manager's personal goals could include retirement after a long career with one company. To honor the manager, a big party would be thrown with work friends and family in attendance. People would travel from great distances at their own expense to be a part of the celebration, which could be acknowledging thirty, forty, and even fifty years of service.

I still remember the first retirement party I attended. The celebration was held in honor of my first mentor. The event was filled with great career stories, lots of laughter, and tender recollections that brought tears to many eyes. Those who attended were not simply work acquaintances; they were his work family. It was a time when employees felt a strong sense of camaraderie as everyone worked for the good of the company.

Much has changed. Companies now attempt to instill teamwork through holding seminars where a manager is told to fall backwards off a step and to depend on a group of work acquaintances to catch her. In our fast-moving work society, farewell lunches have replaced retirement dinners. I cannot think of any managers with whom I've interacted who are ending their management careers with the same company they started out with.

How Long is Too Long?

One of my first reporting relationships was to the advertising manager of a company. He gave me some unsolicited counsel that good managers change jobs every three years. At the time that the manager gave me this piece of career advice, he had been in the same position with the same company for ten years and he ended up staying with that company until it closed its doors. Needless to say, I did not choose him for my mentor support team. His words did not match his actions.

I know of a high-tech company on the West Coast where managers receive a pin with a diamond on it for five years of service. Only a few managers stay long enough to receive a service award for ten years. A particular woman manager transferred to that office from the East Coast facility where company tenure was valued. When she received her award for fifteen years of service, the less tenured managers criticized her for staying with the company too long. The corporate culture was such that the managers decided that she must not be all that good since she wasn't wooed away by another company.

I spent a number of years in an industry where ten or twenty years of experience with the company was valued and rewarded, even within the selling team—which is a highly unusual circumstance for most industries. However, as the market needs changed and evolved, tenure became a liability. Fresh, young sales people just out of college who stayed only a few years but who worked at high intensity became the preferred profile. Managers with ten or more years of experience with the company were tagged as the "old guard," even if they were keeping up with industry changes. If a woman knows that the new management team refers to her with a label that begins with the word "old," it's time to move on.

How Long Is Long Enough?

A woman's career can be negatively affected if she leaves too quickly. When I was a sales director, I regularly reviewed volumes of résumés. When seeking a candidate for a sales position, I would weed out what I refer to as "jumpers." Jumpers are applicants who move from job to job with one or two years of tenure per position. I learned a painful, but valuable lesson when, against my better judgement, I made an offer to a jumper under pressure from my manager. The jumper accepted, attended training, and then resigned, giving only one day's notice, having been on the job less than two months. The jumper will have a difficult time explaining such a short time of employment when interviewing for future positions.

Different industries have different acceptable job change standards. As a senior level manager, I watched carefully for applications from candidates who had a series of job changes that not only weren't promotions but which also indicated a number of slides down various chutes. Those résumés were typically filed away rarely getting a second glance. If I were hiring a customer service manager, I looked for a commitment to previous companies of five to seven years. When hiring for a sales position, the time of service I would look for differed depending on the climate of the particular company. If my company had a weak sales training program, I looked for seasoned reps with five to ten years of tenure. If the company had an effective sales training program, I might hire recent college graduates who were looking to work hard to establish their reputations.

A woman needs to watch her chosen industry carefully and to manage the timing of job changes as close to acceptable industry or position norms as she can. She won't win her personal career game if her goal is to be the last player left on the board.

Time to Go

In their heart of hearts, career women who stay too long know that it's been time to go for a while. A longtime middle manager expressed the following to me:

> *"Things at work are not enjoyable. In fact, mostly I feel frustration. My career has been on a bungee cord, with some nice assignments and rewarding management positions followed by unexplained assignments to one or another 'doghouse' during an ill-thought-out reorganization."*

When a woman uses words and phrases like "not enjoyable, frustration, career on a bungee cord, doghouse," and "ill-thought-out," it's more than time to go. If a woman takes no action when in a frustrating career situation, she positions herself for a career slide.

The Signs Are There

I was downsized after a number of years with a company. As friends and family learned the news, the most frequently asked question was, "Did you see it coming?" Yes, I did. The signs were there.

There are always signs. There are positive signs of company growth that indicate advancement potential for a woman's career. There are signs within catastrophic and chaotic situations that produce opportunity. But there are also signs that indicate that a ride down a chute is in a woman's near future.

I know many women who think that if they only hold on a little longer in disintegrating circumstances, things will turn for the better. If a woman manager ignores the signs, she will likely limit her choices.

Telltale signs include, but are not limited to the following:

- Her funding or operating budget has been heavily cut.
- Her boss and her peers begin to hold strategy meetings without her.
- Her boss becomes either unusually friendly towards her or begins to distance him or herself from her.
- Selected peers begin to distance themselves from her.
- She receives a poor review that differs considerably from past good reviews.
- The number of closed-door meetings escalates and she is not included in them.
- Most of her discussions and interactions with her boss become negative experiences.
- A new management team takes over key positions.
- The company makes a big change in direction and her skill set is no longer a fit for the new plan.
- The company promises opportunity and/or bonuses that never materialize.
- The company has few if no successfully launched new products.
- The company's sales have been flat or declining for several years.
- She reports to a new layer of management placed between her and her former boss

Ignoring these signs ultimately limits a woman's career options.

Taking Action

*"I hate my job. I hate going in to work,
and I'm doing something about it."*

The woman manager who made this statement to me had just come to the realization that she had stayed too long. She had just completed her college degree in hopes of advancement with her present employer. However, she realized that she was witnessing a growing list of injustices at her place of employment. As a human resources manager, she alerted department heads regularly that favoritism was impacting decisions on employees being selected for downsizing. She felt as though she was trying to fight a forest fire of injustices with little more than a garden hose.

She decided to take action and make a career change. She applied for a position near her hometown with a company with which she had been previously employed some years before. She now had a greater value proposition to offer to the company, having both a college degree as well as outside experience to offer.

She explained to me that even though she would be taking a salary cut in making a job change, no amount of money was worth the negativism and unfair practices that she had to endure each day at her present place of employment. She felt that her current circumstances were having a negative impact on her health. To her credit, she took action and got back to the business of managing her career.

Leave at the Top

A woman avoids staying too long when she leaves a company at the top of her game. She will be most marketable after a year in which she has met both the company and her personal goals during difficult market conditions. She is less marketable during years when market conditions erode causing her to miss her goals. Staying too long limits the number and quality of opportunities that will be available to her.

At a point in time, I had just completed a year when I met or exceeded every personal and company goal for which I was responsible. It was invigorating. But I saw a dark cloud forming quickly on the horizon. As it moved closer, I saw a big sign that indicated that a job change would be appropriate.

The company was restructuring and changing direction. The strategy shifts were significant and could only result in declining sales and ultimately some sort of company downsizing. I analyzed the possible impact of the pending downsize as it related to my position and determined that there were three probable outcomes:

1. I could be part of the downsizing, after which I could leverage the severance policy.
2. I could make it through the downsizing, in which case I would most likely be required to take a less challenging position.

3. I could look for a new position with another company, a compelling option since local competitors were looking for people with my background to fill key management positions.

I was in a unique life position at the time wherein any of the three possible outcomes would have been more than workable. The downsizing came quickly, and I became part of it. In my outcome analysis process, I had underestimated just one thing: the positive life changes that the downsizing opportunity would provide. The severance package that I accepted provided sufficient income as I considered how this newly found freedom could propel my life and career in new directions. I grabbed a new ladder and started climbing.

When It Happens

Sometimes there can be few signs and little warning before a woman leader is downsized. When it happens, one of the most career-affecting truths that she should remember is this:

People will always remember how a woman conducts herself as she leaves.

The moment when a woman in management is told that her position has been eliminated can be a difficult one. If she has prepared herself for the possibility of a layoff, she will be able to exhibit self-control. If she has not planned for her next career step in the event of a company downsizing, she may be overwhelmed by emotions and may have difficulty controlling feelings of despair and especially her anger.

I know managers who sabotaged their ability to obtain a reference from a company because they behaved unprofessionally when they were the recipients of the news that their job was eliminated. Some of them angrily walked out, threatening a lawsuit. One manager called every executive at the corporate level to "spill the beans" on several members of the executive staff. There was no impact made. The corporate executives viewed the telephone calls from this manager as just sour grapes. The manager will have a difficult time finding someone within the company who will be willing to give a good work reference for future employment.

Limiting the Choices

I have found that when a company begins to downsize its operations, things go from bad to worse. An initial downsizing usually leads to others. One thing is consistent:

The good packages go first.

Those who decide to stay and ride out the bad times often believe that the company will reward them for picking up the additional workload of those who have been laid off. My experience is that it rarely works that way.

A woman acquaintance recently completed her degree and began seeking her first management position within her company. Unfortunately, the company was acquired and began downsizing at the same time. She declined the opportunity to move on with her boss, which would have meant postponing her management goal for a while longer, but would have gotten her into a new opportunity to position herself for advancement. She also declined the first layoff package by answering the call for volunteers who would stay to turn out the lights. She ended up with a smaller severance package and found herself job hunting in the middle of summer, without success. She told me that in retrospect, she should have taken the first layoff offer.

Another company decided to cut costs by eliminating a number of jobs before a takeover attempt was completed. Several managers who knew of the impending layoffs negotiated packages and left the company. Remaining managers were promised that if they would hang in to wrap things up, they would be taken care of. The new company who overtook the failing company viewed such promises as ones it didn't have to honor, and rescinded many of the severance offerings, leaving loyal managers with loss of income and bitter feelings.

A woman sabotages her career when she volunteers to be the one who turns out the lights when the company closes. She misses the best of any packages offered as well as the widest window of opportunity for reemployment as jobs start going to her counterparts who got out early. She forfeits management of her career and becomes dependent upon the whim of senior managers who are leading a failing company.

Taking Control

The Guidebook states that "for everything there is a season" (Ecclesiastes 3:1a). We are likely to have various work experiences for a limited amount of time. To prepare for new challenges in a new season, a woman needs to actively manage her career and not wait until her employer tells her that her services are no longer needed.

A woman manages her career by continuously watching for new company strategy and assessing how she can leverage her knowledge, skills, and abilities within that strategy. She regularly reviews her available opportunities to determine if her best career move is to continue with her current company or to look for employment elsewhere. A woman who is managing her career continues to develop and strengthen her transferable skills. Her résumé is up to date and ready for use to apply for positions both outside as well as inside her current organization.

A woman will be able to release her grip on her current ladder rung so that she can reach for the next one when she carefully manages the timing of her next move.

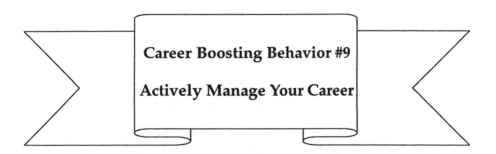

Career Boosting Behavior #9

Actively Manage Your Career

In Closing

If this book has produced a desire to address behaviors that may be sabotaging your career, I encourage you with this thought:

When the captain of a cruise ship that is traveling at normal cruising speed cuts the engines, the ship will travel a full mile before it will come to a complete stop so that the ship can reverse course.

Change does not occur instantaneously. It requires time, deliberate action, and a vision for what you want your career to be. A woman who chooses to root out and change career-sabotaging behaviors will discover more career ladders and will reduce her chances of tumbling down hidden chutes.

A woman in leadership has accepted a high calling. It is one that compels her to live a life of integrity, balance, and vision. In closing, I borrow a verse from the Guidebook that expresses my hope for every woman leader:

I urge you to live a life worthy of the calling you have received.
—Ephesians 4:1

CAREER BOOSTING BEHAVIORS

✓ Leverage Your Uniqueness

✓ Treat Male Colleagues as Customers

✓ Create and Use a Mentor Support Team

✓ Be a Mentor

✓ Hold Your Professional Image to a High Standard

✓ Take the Positive Perspective

✓ Base Life and Career on the Same Core Values

✓ Embrace Risk

✓ Actively Manage Your Career

BVG